The Holy Spirit & Preaching

*Dedicated to the
memory of
my mother*
MABLE CLEMONS FORBES
1912 - 1969

and

*to the magnificent ministry
of my father*
BISHOP JAMES A. FORBES, SR.

ACKNOWLEDGMENTS

I wish to express my gratitude to the many seminaries, ministers' conferences and workshops for giving me the opportunity to engage in dialogue concerning "things of the spirit."

Special thanks is due my colleagues at Union Theological Seminary and Auburn Seminary for their gifts of friendship and loving criticality in service of "a more excellent way."

For his many hours of personal and professional advice, Professor James M. Washington deserves more appreciation than can be expressed in this limited space.

Robin Lytle Turner, my editorial assistant, gave more than faithful service. Her prayers and encouragement helped to sustain the project.

I am especially grateful for the patience, persistence and editorial wisdom of Greg Michael, the Professional Books Editor at Abingdon Press, who shared in this project as a God given companion along the way.

Finally I must acknowledge that my wife, Bettye, and my son, James - through their support and longing to see the completion of this book - provided the motivation and companionship I needed to "bring forth."

CONTENTS

INTRODUCTION

The invitation to deliver the Lyman Beecher Lectures of 1986 at Yale Divinity School provided a special opportunity for me to bring together two special interests. The first was to share in an ecumenical setting the fruit of many years of reflection on Holy Spirit renewal in the life of the church. The second was to identify and present the most significant contribution I could offer for the enrichment of preaching. These two areas represent dimensions of ministry that have claimed my interest and vocational energy for more than twenty-five years. In selecting a theme for the lectureship, it became clear that both concerns led to a single focus - the Holy Spirit and preaching.

The decision to focus on this subject reflects a strong and growing conviction: if a greatly improved quality of preaching is to be experienced in our time, it will stem from the renewing power and presence of the Holy Spirit. Similarly, Holy Spirit renewal in the life of the church will increase significantly as more powerful preaching is heard from our pulpits.

As I begin this ecumenical conversation on Holy Spirit renewal and the empowerment of preaching, it may be helpful to discuss the context out of which these concerns emerged and how they've come to hold a central place in my own teaching and preaching.

My longing to engage in serious conversation about Holy Spirit renewal across denominational lines was sparked during the early days of my seminary education at Union Theological Seminary in New York.

I arrived at the seminary in September of 1958, though I had applied a year earlier. During the year of waiting, one of the bishops of my church (The United Holy Church of America) questioned the wisdom of exposing myself to the liberalism and biblical criticism for which Union was so well-known. He feared that I might "lose" the Holy Spirit - if not my faith altogether - in such an environment. Moreover, he wondered whether there would be acceptance and appreciation for the faith experience I brought out of the black southern Pentecostal religion.

My apprehension was diminished significantly in June of 1958, when *Life* magazine published an article by H. Pitney Van Dusen, then president of Union Seminary. His article was entitled "Pentecostalism - The Third Force in Christendom." Dr. Van Dusen had been impressed with the vibrancy and rapid growth of Pentecostal churches in Central and South America. He thought these Pentecostal sects reflected in their worship the contagious power of New Testament times. Indeed, he wondered if mainline churches might not discover in the dynamic of these churches something vital, though missing, in their more traditional forms of worship and general piety.

The article came at a most opportune time. I arrived at the seminary confident there would be respect for my tradition. I was not disappointed. In fact, many faculty members and students showed interest and expressed hope that I would not lose the richness of my unique religious experience. They believed the Pentecostal tradition was on to something essential to vital Christianity. I recall an occasion when Reinhold Niebuhr had lunch with a group of us incoming students. Upon learning of my background, he warned me not to let seminary training rob me of the fervency of my Pentecostal heritage.

In the midst of my studies of the classical theological disciplines, my conviction that the experience of the Holy Spirit was crucial to the revitalization of the church was reinforced. I read with excitement President Van Dusen's book *Spirit, Son and Father*. It was subtitled *Christian Faith in the Light of the Holy Spirit.*

The power, pastoral sensitivity, and insight into Christian struggle reflected in Paul Tillich's sermon "Spiritual Presence" convinced me that he knew something about the Spirit I had experienced in prayer meetings back home at Providence Holy Church in Raleigh, North Carolina. Portions of Tillich's third volume of *Systematic Theology* were presented as a part of the Monday morning lecture series in James Chapel at the seminary. I didn't fully understand his accent or concepts, but I sensed the majesty and mystery of the Spirit and its place in his monumental theological system. Following those lectures, I began calling myself a Tillichian Pentecostal.

I saw in James Muilenburg's Old Testament classes and John Knox's New Testament lectures and in Bill Webber's East Harlem Protestant Parish ministry, manifestations of the Spirit in living color. Their forms and styles of expression were different than mine, but I sensed the same Spirit inspiring us all.

As I gained broader exposure, I observed that some of the ingredients for spiritual awareness were missing in the larger church. I saw theoretical familiarity without experiential concreteness. The noticeable absence of freedom in liturgical expression often left me cold and unfulfilled. There also seemed to be little awareness of the biblical gifts of the Spirit - at least the ones that were talked about in my church. Although I couldn't be certain, it seemed there was little reliance upon the power of the Spirit for the work of ministry. There definitely was not the general acknowledgment of such a dependency - if it was indeed a part of the faith understanding. There were exceptions, but I became convinced that the exchange of views and broadening of experiences would be profitable for both sides of the theological and ecclesiastical divide.

In preparing my Bachelor of Divinity thesis in 1962, I reflected upon what I felt was an emerging sense of vocation. The topic was "Pentecostalism and the Renewal of the Church." I had been challenged by the observation of Lesslie Newbigin, then the Bishop of the Church of South India, in his book *The Household of God*: "I believe that the

13

Catholic-Protestant debate which has characterized the ecumenical movement needs to be criticized and supplemented from what I have called the Pentecostal angle, that in fact the debate has to become three-cornered" (page 102).

I also was impressed by the work of David Du Plessis, a South African Pentecostal who felt a special call to share his witness in ecumenical circles. I had heard of his conversations regarding the place of the Spirit in the broader Christian world. This seemed to reinforce my own sense of calling for ecumenical ministry.

Since then, my ministry has involved searching for ways to help the larger church community experience the empowerment found in the Pentecostal emphasis on the experience of the Holy Spirit.

In this work, I hope to set forth what I have learned and to promote a comprehensive ecumenical conversation on the renewal of the church in the power of the Holy Spirit.

I also hope to show how contemporary preaching can be enriched by a fresh appropriation of the power of the Holy Spirit. I strongly believe that an effective call to Holy Spirit empowerment is a most valuable homiletical offering.

I have been a student of preaching most of my life. According to family lore, as a preschool lad I used to stand on a coffee table to imitate my father's fiery preaching style. Throughout my childhood I was surrounded by preachers. My grandfather, grandmother, several uncles, an aunt, and of course my father all were preachers. Much of my youth was spent listening to one of these preachers or observing a host of ministers at various conferences, convocations, revivals, and assorted district meetings.

After many years of resisting the call to become a preacher, I finally accepted the vocation during my junior year at Howard University. As I prepared for my ministry, I became most interested in hearing outstanding pulpiteers. I rarely missed an opportunity to be inspired by the preaching of the likes of Bishop H. H. Hairton, Mordecai Johnson, Vernon Johns, Howard Thurman, Gardner C. Taylor, Adam Clayton Powell, Jr., Samuel Procter, and Martin Luther King, Jr.

Years later, after graduating from Union, four congregations provided contexts in which I began to observe how
diverse congregations experience and call forth the gift of
preaching in their ministers. The first summer after gradu-
ation was spent at the Olin T. Binkley Memorial (Southern)
Baptist Church in Chapel Hill, North Carolina, under the
leadership of Dr. Robert J. Seymour, whose excellent
manuscript preaching and personal witness inspired church
members to extraordinary faithfulness for justice and
equality in their community.

I later served three congregations of my own denomination: Holy Trinity Church, Wilmington, North Carolina; St.
Paul Holy Church, Roxboro, North Carolina; and St. John
Holy Church, Richmond, Virginia. It was always a bit
strange to my church members to hear a Tillichian Pentecostal proclaiming the gospel with a curious combination
of heart and head. Indeed, I often felt the tension between
the old-time religion and the new-age perspective that I
was attempting to embody. Nevertheless, in each of the
churches I received support from seasoned saints and
growing numbers of young people as well. I encouraged
worship and fellowship with churches of other denominations and sought to lead my members to translate the
warmth of spirit we experienced into vibrant witness in the
community. I came to characterize our style of ministry as
"progressive pentecostalism" - a strong emphasis on spirit,
but deep commitment to transformative social action. This
has been a continuing emphasis for me, both in congregational leadership and in seminary teaching.

My years at Union have strengthened my ecumenical
journey with the Spirit. The seminary's diversity is like a
theological United Nations. There was a strong emphasis
on respect for various traditions and cultures, which helped
me recognize the many different ways the Spirit ministers
in the church.

I highly value the insights I gained from this exposure.
In my teaching and preaching, I seek to reflect the benefits
of this experience. At the same time, I see the need for
sharing the perspective and emphases of my own tradition. I am convinced that vast improvements in preaching

15

can be expected if, in addition to traditional preparation for the preaching ministry, more attention is given to the process by which preachers are endowed with the Holy Spirit for the work they are called to do.

It is out of this pilgrimage that I have come to the convictions which are reflected in this work - *the anointing makes the difference!*

The anointing of the Holy Spirit is the central paradigm for our discussion. It is a biblical category with rich experiential meaning. The hope is that as the whole church discovers provisions for empowerment and guidance, we will enter into a new season of revitalization and renewal.

Throughout this book, a strong emphasis will be placed on the conditions for achieving ecumenical conversation. Obviously, there are many aspects of Christian action and experience that may be pursued within the confines of particular congregations and denominations. The purpose of this effort is to make the case that the spiritual renewal needed today must involve intercommunion and interdenominational cooperation. We must recognize that forces at work in our culture to limit the spiritual dynamic of church life require concerted opposition from all church traditions. The fragmentation and separation in the body of Christ is part of the malaise to be overcome. This is especially the case in the conflicting views of how the Holy Spirit is to be experienced in the church today.

Until we come together humbly to try to understand the causes of our divisions and the diminished faithfulness of our witness, our renewal will be delayed. On the other hand, we can expect to see the manifestation of the gifts of the Spirit in new ways if we jointly seek God's remediating grace.

Let us consider what we can do to hasten the coming of that day of more vibrant faith.

In chapter 1, there will be a discussion of the need for renewed emphasis on the relationship between the Holy Spirit and preaching. The anointing of the Holy Spirit in the life of Jesus will be presented as a model of spiritual formation for the ministry of preaching. Chapters 2 and 3 focus on the anointing in the life of Jesus and the difference the anointing can make in our own preaching ministries - in terms of both concept and content. Chapter 4 will describe how the anointing may become a revitalizing experience for the church in our time.

PREACHING AND
THE HOLY SPIRIT

The person who preaches the gospel makes a statement about the Holy Spirit just by entering the pulpit. Even before the first word is uttered, presuppositions and definitions from across the centuries speak volumes about the Spirit-led event to be experienced by the preacher and the community of worshipers. The preaching event itself - without reference to specific texts and themes - is a living, breathing, flesh-and-blood expression of the theology of the Holy Spirit.

Consider how the Holy Spirit has been at work to make possible the traditional preaching situation: It is the Spirit who has inspired the scripture lessons of the day. It is the Spirit who has shepherded the word through compilation, translation, canonization, and transmission to the present time. It is the Spirit who convenes a congregation to hear the word of God. And it is the Spirit who opens our hearts and minds to receive anew God's self-disclosure as the living word.

The preaching event is an aspect of the broader work of the Spirit to nurture, empower, and guide the church in order that it may serve the kingdom of God in the power of the Spirit. It is a process in which the divine-human communication is activated and focused on the word of God and is led by a member of the community of faith who has been called, anointed, and appointed by the Holy Spirit to be an agent of divine communication. That person's authority is grounded in the self-revealing will of God as articulated and elaborated in the biblical witness. In addition, the preacher's authority is confirmed or ordained by the community of faith in response to the continuing counsel of the Holy Spirit.

Such pneumatological affirmations reflect the general understanding of a vast majority of Christians, with the emphasis being on Holy Spirit presence and action in the congregational settings where the preaching takes place.

Given this understanding, it seems to follow that the quality of the preaching is affected most significantly by the level of awareness of the movement of the Spirit shared by those in the pulpit and pew.

Although the church generally has subscribed to this view, the proper place of the Holy Spirit has been neglected in its life and work. Indeed, the history of the church records a pattern of ebb and flow of its attentiveness to the ministry of the Spirit. Sometimes various communities are in states of vigorous excitement, mild acceptance, or benign neglect of the Spirit as the vital source of strength and guidance for the life of the church. It is only through periodic renewal and recovery of spiritual depth that the power and grace of the Holy Spirit actually can be appropriated.

In *A History of Preaching*, Edwin Dargan draws on his comprehensive review of preaching through the centuries to make this general observation regarding the life of the Spirit and the quality of preaching:

> Decline of spiritual life and activity in the churches is commonly accompanied by a lifeless, formal, unfruitful preaching, and this partly as cause, partly as effect. On the other hand, the great revivals of Christian history can most usually be traced to the work of the pulpit, and in their progress they have developed and rendered possible a high order of preaching. (Vol. 1, page 13)

During recent years, we have seen some signs of spiritual revitalization. Still, it would be premature to celebrate the arrival of the long-awaited renewal. While we have heard periodic declarations about how the church is on the threshold of a spiritual revival, it seems evident that a considerable breakup of old patterns and perspectives is necessary before a significant breakthrough can come.

We can hope and pray that each aspect of the life and ministry of the church will be open to the revitalization the Spirit seeks to bring - especially in the area of preaching.

Jesus came preaching in the power of the Spirit. He shared with his disciples his awareness of power, rooted and grounded in God, which was at work in him and in the context in which he ministered.

The great prophets of Israel who came before Jesus also proclaimed, "Thus saith the Lord," as the Spirit moved them. They addressed their times out of a definite sense of divine appointment and empowerment.

The Apostles, whom Jesus initiated into the continuing work of the kingdom, were told to expect the coming of the Spirit, in whose power they were to bear witness to Jesus. Through the centuries, enthusiasts, as well as guardians of institutional forms of ministry, have found ways to account for that mysterious presence which touched their efforts with grace.

To preach today in Jesus' name, and to do so with power, still requires the enabling presence of the Holy Spirit. I do not know a conscientious preacher anywhere who would claim to preach without at least some acknowledgment of the aid of the Spirit, even if the minister did not tend to speak of it in that way. There are many preachers who are waiting for and depending on the power from beyond themselves - and there are many who are aware that if that power is not present, the preaching will not be effective.

Increasingly, clergy and lay persons are hearing more about the Spirit. Their sources may be television, periodicals, evangelists or church members who attend charismatic conferences. But many Christians are Holy Spirit—shy. For some, conversations about empowerment of the

Spirit in one's ministry are occasions of anxiety and intimidation. Some preachers hesitate to speak of the Spirit in relationship to what they do. Others talk about the Spirit in traditional language of faith, but without personal meaning. Hence, many of the biblical provisions for Holy Spirit empowerment often are left unrealized like unclaimed packages or unopened letters.

In the church and society today, there are forces working to prevent us from fully receiving the power of the Spirit for preaching. Let us consider some of the reasons why preachers often feel the need to avoid Holy Spirit language and why many steer clear of claiming the Spirit as the power at the heart of their preaching.

In our secular, post modern age, we risk appearing unsophisticated if there is too much talk about a spiritual dimension of reality, or if we make too much space for the presence and activity of the Spirit in our day-to-day experiences. In fact, in some traditions there are well-defined, sacramental systems that rigidly insist that all talk of the experience of the Spirit be limited to the official means of grace. Even though word and sacrament are always appropriately viewed under the Spirit's guidance, we are cautioned against hints of enthusiasm or special, personal unctions. Sometimes ecclesiastical leaders fear that private and personal spiritual visitations will lead to excesses and potential conflict in the community of believers.

In other places there is reticence about referring to the Holy Spirit because of doctrinal positions and stereotyped manifestations, to which some ministers take serious exception. Some preachers would rather avoid discussing the Holy Spirit altogether lest they be understood in terms of popular notions that aren't consistent with their own doctrinal views, or that reflect reductionist understandings.

Often, mainline Christians are willing to leave the Spirit-talk as a special vocation for the Spirit-filled folks. "Let them talk that way," they may say. In such a response, avoidance of Holy Spirit themes or references are intended to defend against what could be exaggerated or distorted claims.

But there is another reason why some of us shy away from the Spirit. Many of us fear being grasped by an invisible presence we cannot control. In this regard, we share the problematics of spiritual experience throughout all ages.

We may wonder, "What am I likely to do? How will I behave if I surrender my control to the Divine Spirit? How can I be sure that some other spirit won't actually take over my mind?" Rudolf Otto in *Idea of the Holy* (pages 12-13) calls this strange feeling of attraction and dread "mysterium tremendum." It is the awe-filled experience of the majesty of God - overpowering and yet enrapturing - both thrilling and chilling. But it nevertheless envelopes the longing for the Spirit with deep emotive ambiguity. In any event, respectful distance - not only from experiencing the Spirit, but also from language about the Holy Spirit - may seem to be the better part of wisdom, especially for moderns who are given to quantification and control. Consequently, the Holy Spirit is less understood, less experienced, and doesn't have a meaningful place in the world view or the sacred cosmos of most of us.

In his book *Christian Spirituality* (page 83), Wolfhart Pannenberg accounts for this trend by noting that in the "death of God" generation there was a philosophical and theological statement of the lost sense of spirit perception, but what we have now is an actual, existential living out of the fact that God's presence in the world, active in form of Spirit, is not a normal perception for most of us today.

Louis Dupre in *Spiritual Life in a Secular Age* makes a similar observation as he describes experiences of the Spirit in our secular age. He maintains that the ability to experience the sacred and to have some immediate sense of its authenticity has eroded for most people. No matter what we experience, our way of thinking requires us to try to give a scientific explanation of the factors that could have contributed to the phenomenon in question. And if we are led to affirm that an experience was caused by the presence of the Spirit, we take on the added burden of seeking its verification as we live out the implications of the faith claim we have made. Dupre says, "In our time, the religious interpretation comes as a result of further reflection, and only rarely with the experience itself. Since the interpretation remains separate from the experience, the doubt about its correctness can be resolved only by a subsequent, full commitment to it. Hence the experience receives its definitive meaning only in its final, voluntary act of assent" (page 5). All the while we hope that life's experiences will corroborate our spiritual sensitivity so that we can joyfully say, "Surely, that was the work of the Holy Spirit in my life." In a secular society, such affirmations become more difficult to make. This fact may be a persisting problematic of most serious proportions for spiritual development in our age.

Indeed, Dupre makes a disturbing observation which should be a source of special concern for those who serve in religious vocations.

> The search for a deeper spiritual life is, in fact, more than a passing phenomenon on today's religious scene; it is a movement for religious survival. For without the support of a sustained personal decision, a religion that remains unassisted by the surrounding culture and is constantly under attack in the believer's own heart is doomed to die.... The doctrines, lifestyles and methods of a previous age were conceived within the reach of a direct experience of the sacred. This has for the most part ceased to exist. (page 13)

I am convinced that Pentecostals and charismatics, as well as mainline Christians - be they conservative or liberal - face a common problem. Given the predominating view of reality in which we live, many find it difficult to know with certainty that it is indeed the Spirit of the Lord who shapes our personal and religious experience. Even those who have that deep and abiding certainty about the action of the Spirit in their lives sometimes find they too question the justification for their strong affirmation.

It is about this general problem that I write because I believe it isn't just a minority of people who are Spirit-shy. My sense is that most of us find it difficult to experience the sacred - which may explain why the high calling to live out the mandates of the kingdom (righteousness, justice, joy, and peace) finds decreasing compliance. To rise above preoccupation with, or fixation on, our own interests, or to respond to the mandate to give to others, presupposes strong assurances about Holy Spirit support.

To live as if we could indeed trust God places a strain on all who live in the time of scientific verification. If the religious foundation, the sense of the sacred, the visitation of the Spirit no longer is real for us, then we would begin to expect that the secular domination of our thought patterns would render moral and ethical patterns of life subject to steady decline. Given this situation, it would seem that the church as a whole shares the need to search for ways by which we may be in touch once again with the power of the Spirit.

If we intend to preach the gospel of Jesus the Christ, who calls us to serve the kingdom in our time, we need all the power that is available to us. Given the reality of a culture that has lost contact with the living Spirit of the one who announced to us the vision of the kingdom in the first place, we need preaching that is more than aesthetically delightful. Mere ranting and raving and excitation from some spirited pastor will not suffice. We need some sense of the Spirit accompanied by power sufficient to interrupt a decline in the sense of the reality of God.

Paul's testimony captures the sense of what is needed in our time:

> When I came to you, brethren, I did not come proclaiming to you the testimony of God in lofty words or wisdom. For I decided to know nothing among you except Jesus Christ and him crucified. And I was with you in weakness and in much fear

and trembling; and my speech and my message were not in plausible words of wisdom, but in demonstration of the Spirit and of power, that your faith might not rest in the wisdom of humankind, but in the power of God. (I Cor. 2: 1-5)

The primary issue here is not how much one talks about the Spirit. Rather, the concern is that those forces that reduce our freedom to speak of the Holy Spirit also may be working against any diligence in seeking the guidance and the empowerment of the Spirit. It is not that preachers do not know the place of the Spirit. Rather, it is that those attitudes which urge silence or privacy regarding the role of the Spirit in our preaching also tend to rob us of the full empowerment crucial for all who preach the Word. Barriers to such anointings are very real and need to be faced if we are to experience additional dimensions of Holy Spirit power for more effective preaching.

What might it mean for preachers today if when we stand to preach we could say, "The Spirit of the Lord is upon us, because the Lord hath anointed us to preach the gospel"? This is the question at the heart of our quest. It is my goal that preachers all over this nation, regardless of their denominational background, piety, or theological perspective in general, would be able, with integrity, to say, "The Spirit of the Lord is upon me, because the Lord has anointed me for the preaching of the gospel."

There is a way in which all of the church can experience the reality of the Spirit. The decline in the sense of the spiritual presence reflected in our age may be confronted by a new power in the life of the church. Let us seek that way by focusing on the anointing of the Holy Spirit in the life of Jesus.

The Anointing of Jesus

The anointing of Jesus can be viewed as a model of spiritual formation. If experientially appropriated, this same anointing will promote a renewal of the awareness of the Holy Spirit and the empowerment necessary for more effective preaching.

Once we understand more clearly what this anointing means and stand under its continuing influence, we will observe a marked difference in the way we preach, and the objectives of the gospel will be manifested more abundantly.

In conducting preaching workshops and conferences across the country, I have spoken with many members of the clergy and laity who have expressed eagerness to probe more deeply into the implications of the concept of anointing. Their questions reveal sharp differences of opinion about how the Spirit equips the church for ministry today. The development of the ideas presented here is in large measure an attempt to think through the many perplexing problems that have been discussed in ecumenical settings.

While we could profitably consider what effect the anointing has on various aspects of ministry, it is hoped that by focusing on preaching, the larger inquiry will be stimulated.

Jesus came to Nazareth. He unrolled the Scriptures and found the place where it was written, "The Spirit of the Lord is upon me, because he has anointed me to preach good news to the poor" (Luke 4:18). He then gave the scroll to the attendant, took his seat, and said, "Today this scripture has been fulfilled in your hearing" (verse 21).

In Jesus' use of the text, it is clear that he was making some kind of claim about himself, the nature of his mission, and the kingdom he came to announce. His use of Isaiah 61 as the basis of his ministry - quoting these words that are so familiar to all of us - should be instructive for us. The question to be raised is, "What did Jesus mean by the words, 'because the Lord has anointed me'"? What specific meaning can be affirmed when Jesus said, "The Spirit of the Lord is upon me because he has anointed me"?

In general, the verb "to anoint" by biblical definition means to pour, rub, or to spread, as an ointment, an oil, or a fragrance. Such could function either as religious ritual, or medicinally, or cosmetically. But the basic idea is that when this special ointment was used, something significant happened. In most cases the basic intent symbolizes and concretizes divine authorization, within religious ritual. It gives evidence of the impartation of wisdom and knowledge, and the communication of the grace and power of God. Such persons who were so anointed, by virtue of their anointing, were expected to serve as representatives of God in whose name and power they were so anointed.

An interesting passage reflecting the multiple uses of the term can be found in Exodus 30:22-33:

> Moreover, the Lord said to Moses, "Take the finest spices: of liquid myrrh five hundred shekels, and of sweet-smelling cinnamon half as much, that is, two hundred and fifty, and of aromatic cane two hundred and fifty, and of cassia five hundred, according to the shekel of the sanctuary, and of olive oil a hin; and you shall make of these a sacred anointing oil blended as by the perfumer; a holy anointing oil it shall be. And you shall anoint with it the tent of meeting and the ark of the testimony, and the table and all its utensils, and the lampstand and its utensils, and the altar of incense, and the altar of burnt offering with all its utensils and the laver and its base; you shall consecrate them, that they may be most holy; whatever touches them will become holy. And you shall anoint Aaron and his sons, and consecrate them, that they may serve me as priests. And you shall say to the people of Israel, 'This shall be my holy anointing oil throughout your generations. It shall not be poured upon the bodies of ordinary men, and you shall make no other like it in composition; it is holy, and it shall be holy to you. Whoever compounds any like it or whoever puts any of it on an outsider shall be cut off from his people.'"

Notice that the items that were to be used in religious ritual, and even the people who were to serve, were to have the holy anointing oil. This is a special, holy anointing oil. It was not to be used for non sacred purposes. The formula was given by God. And anyone who took it lightly was to be separated from the community.

In the course of the development of the concept of the anointing, it came to be identified with the restoration of power and might, by which the servant of the Lord would usher in the age to come. Isaiah is frequently quoted to link the anointing of the Spirit with the "coming one." There is some ambiguity in these renderings as to whether that means the whole people of God, or a person of God who will be anointed in the New Age. However, in Joel 2, it is clearly announced that all flesh shall be the recipient of the pouring, the anointing of the Spirit.

In the fourth chapter of Luke, when Jesus stands to speak of his anointing, his action and his speech either explicitly indicated he was the Anointed One, or gave rise to the church's affirmation of Jesus as the Anointed One.

In traditions where the language of anointings has been used, the discussion has tended to be identified with a particular one-time experience or a moment of heightened excitement. It also has been related to empowerment for a particular vocation or ministry for healing from a specific illness.

I propose that what Jesus meant by the anointing, as he applied it to himself, is retained by the apostolic tradition. In Peter's sermon at Cornelius's house, the following perspective is given: "You know the word which is sent to Israel, preaching good news of peace by Jesus Christ (he is Lord of all), the word which was proclaimed throughout all Judea, beginning from Galilee after the baptism which John preached: how God anointed Jesus of Nazareth with the Holy Spirit and with power; and how he went about doing good and healing all that were oppressed by the devil, for God was with him" (Acts 10: 36-38).

Although there is the mystery of messianic fulfillment in Jesus of Nazareth, there are indications of what Jesus might have experienced before and following the baptismal experience. These experiences within his community of faith may have confirmed in his consciousness that indeed he was anointed with the Holy Spirit. Perhaps confirmation came from the quality of his nurture in the various communities that had helped him with his self-understanding and his sense of mission. It may have come from a moment of heightened awareness or a series of concentrated encounters, all of which had the cumulative impact of confirming his anointing. Or it may have been a combination of these factors.

As difficult as it is to pinpoint the central features of our own inner experiences, it is even more difficult to identify the central foundational experiences of Jesus. In each of us there is a unique unfolding of God-consciousness that defies analysis because it is safe guarded by the mystery of human interaction within the heart of God. But in the light of details found in the Gospel accounts, several dimensions of growth may be suggested as aspects of the anointing, which is a continuous process.

The first thing to be said about what the anointing might have been in Jesus is the affirmation of his unique relationship to the God whom he chose to call Father. This is foundational to what we can say about the meaning of the anointing. That is, when the church affirms that Jesus is conceived by the Holy Ghost, it is underscoring a singular, unique reality. We do not expect to explain our own biological conception in that way because Jesus is the "only begotten of the Father." According to our faith, every Christian is conceived by the Holy Spirit, but this points to spiritual rebirth.

But in Jesus' conception, we find a very important clue with which to begin our analysis and discussion. For if what we say about the anointing of Jesus begins with his unique relationship, it would very well suggest that the most important beginning for the ecumenical conversation regarding the anointing of the Spirit is to affirm the uniqueness, not only of Jesus' relationship, but the relationship of any one of us with the God whom we call Mother or Father.

There is no way to meaningfully discuss the anointing of the Spirit without acknowledging that all of our lives in relationship with God are unique expressions. There are no clones in the community of faith - not denominationally, nor theologically. Although there is a tendency in every tradition to make strong suggestions regarding prescribed patterns of spiritual formation, there is little to suggest that there is only one approach to spiritual growth. For an ecumenical conversation, individuals must perceive that their counterparts are willing to affirm their faith. Otherwise, the conversation is likely to be skewed from the beginning by defensiveness or inordinate amounts of energy used to ensure mutuality of respect.

It is important that we also rise above the tendency to arrange stages of spiritual growth in rigid patterns of ascending and descending values. How wisely Tillich warned us against the use of "steps" with regard to spiritual growth. His word "dimensions" is preferable because it avoids the temptation to play the game of "I am more anointed than thou." To qualify for the ecumenical conversation about the anointing, we must be able to say "Amen - so let it be" to the God-affirming uniqueness of the lives and growth of others.

Such a requirement has been a problem. In the conversations I have experienced through the years, there has not been sufficient affirmation of the uniqueness of personal relationships to let the conversation go anywhere other than in the direction of greater defense for one's own orientation. I have observed rigidity in various theological circles. Hence, the importance for all of us to examine our attitudes toward other perspectives. That's the first point to be made about the anointing of the Holy Spirit in Jesus's life as well as in ours. Affirmation of the uniqueness of our relationships with God is foundational for all other dimensions of spiritual growth.

Second, the anointing of Jesus cannot be separated from his nurture in his family and in his faith community. In his book *Christian Nurture*, Horace Bushnell alerts us to the power of the atmosphere, instructions, and valuing processes in the formative stages of a person's development. Luke 2:52 gives attention to the growth process in Jesus: "And Jesus increased in wisdom and in stature, and in favor with God and [humankind]."

In reflecting upon Jesus' relationship with Mary, we cannot discount or fail to appreciate what he learned at her knee or by her side. Did her countenance reflect to him the things she pondered in her heart? And consider Jesus' relationship with Joseph. When authorities sought the young boy's life, Joseph acted promptly by taking his family to safety in Egypt. And Jesus, during time spent with Joseph, not only learned about carpentry, but also about his self-identity. It is certain that Jesus' personal and spiritual development were significantly forged by these relationships.

We must abandon the notion of a weekend experience that achieves an overwhelming experience of God, but would deem everything that came before it as absolutely unimportant. Jesus seemed to have spent a prolonged period of nurture. How eager he was, at age twelve, to get on with the business, but the time had not come because it was necessary that the nurturing process continue. So he went home with Mary and Joseph to be under their parental influence.

It is possible that Jesus felt the urge to get on with his ministry at various times during those so-called silent years. Still, he took time to allow circumstances and nurture to come to full fruition.

In addition to parental influence, Jesus was deeply affected by the religious leadership in the synagogue and community. This served as a broader context of nurture. The account of Jesus engaged in conversation with the teachers in the Temple in Jerusalem (Luke 2:41-51) reflects his keen interest in learning from those who were masters of the tradition. It seems altogether plausible that the quality of respect Jesus received from those mentors of the faith awakened a sense of his own destiny.

I imagine a conversation of twelve-year-old Jesus, standing there asking questions of the rabbis: He asked, "Sirs, when will that day come?"

"The day will come when time has been made ready

according to the will of God," one rabbi answered.

"And, how will we know that that time has come?"

"Well," one rabbi said, "one will be sent who will declare unto the world the moment of readiness for all that the people of Israel have waited for through the centuries."

Then, I suppose, Jesus said, "Sirs, how will that person know that he is the one chosen to announce that day?"

Whereupon a rabbi may have responded, "Young man, it may very well be that you will be the one to announce that age."

It should not be surprising to learn that Jesus was annoyed when Mary and Joseph interrupted this conversation of destiny (Luke 2:48). Mary chided him: "Son, why have you treated us so? Behold, your father and I have been looking for you anxiously." And Jesus' prophetic reply: "How is it that you sought me? Did you not know that I must be in my Father's house?" (Luke 2:49).

Who Jesus was to become cannot be separated from the intimations of his mission gained in his childhood and synagogue education.

Though little is known about the religious training of Jesus during his youth, general patterns of his day provide some clues. The so-called silent years (from ages twelve to thirty) have been the subject of much speculation. Nevertheless, we do know that at about age thirty, Jesus had reached the point of vocational readiness - an issue often overlooked in consideration of the anointing of the Spirit. Popular concepts have tended to focus on heartwarming experience for the sake of personal fulfillment, rather than preparation for ministry.

Central to the anointing process, however, is the preparation of persons for the tasks to which they have been called. The emphasis on vocational readiness provides a more helpful point of conversation in ecumenical dialogue. Where the focus is on personal spiritual formation or character development, more narrow and particularistic interests prevail. What this dimension highlights is the importance of moving beyond the ready room like astronauts awaiting launch time. The longing is to come forth to yield ourselves fully to that to which we are called.

Jesus' eagerness to go forth to his task may have placed this sentiment in his heart: "Whatever my life is meant to be, O God, who sent me into the world, let me get on with it. Let me be fully engaged, publicly, in that to which you have called me." It was a time of vocational readiness with such an urgency that he was not willing to accept John's expression of respect, suggesting that he was unworthy of baptizing Jesus. Instead, Jesus insisted, "Let it to be so now . . . " (Matthew 3:15).

For Jesus, readiness manifested itself in obedient action in response to the guidance of the Spirit. Readiness leads to moving out from where we have been to getting on the path of promise . . . the path promised as the source from which one's insight, energy, and guidance will come. Thus Jesus went down to join those who were waiting to be baptized by John in the Jordan River.

Events surrounding the baptism of Jesus are at the heart of the New Testament understanding of the anointing. In Peter's sermon at Cornelius' house, the identification of baptism and Holy Spirit anointing is made.

> "You know the word which he sent to Israel, preaching good news of peace by Jesus Christ (he is Lord of all), the word which was proclaimed throughout all Judea, beginning from Galilee after the baptism which John preached: how God anointed Jesus of Nazareth with the Holy Spirit and with power; how he went about doing good and healing all that were oppressed by the devil, for God was with him." (Acts 10: 36-38)

When John the Baptist consented to baptize Jesus, he was administering an aspect of divine preparation for Jesus' prophetic and messianic vocation. Various schools of thought will offer different interpretations of the sacramental nature of baptism as well as the precise mode or formula to be invoked. A vibrant exchange of ideas on these matters now centers around the World Council of

Churches—sponsored consultation on baptism, eucharist, and ministry. Whatever the outcome of these discussions, the apostolic tradition and the symbolism of immersion, pouring, or sprinkling, all link baptism and anointing in the spiritual formation of Jesus for his salvific work.

But the actual baptism does not constitute the totality of the anointing experience. As Jesus comes up from the waters of the Jordan, we observe two additional dimensions of the anointing: "Now when all the people were baptized, and when Jesus also had been baptized and was praying, the heaven was opened, and the Holy Spirit descended upon him in bodily form, as a dove, and a voice came from heaven, 'Thou art my beloved Son; with thee I am well pleased'" (Luke 3: 21-22).

In this account, Luke identifies the descent of the dove as symbolic of the Holy Spirit coming to rest upon Jesus. This makes available to Jesus, not only the power that had been at work by virtue of his unique relationship, but power from beyond himself. The sense is communicated that the same power that was at work at the beginning of the creation now is flowing through the chosen servant of God. It is the coming together of the power within and the power from beyond that signals a growing sense of the anointing.

Also, when the heaven was opened a voice was heard: Thou art my beloved Son - with thee I am well pleased. At that moment, Jesus experienced divine acceptance, approval, and appointment. There was no need for him to consult with the rabbis or even with Mary about his readiness for ministry. He had heard the word of confirmation from heaven. The work he was called to do would expose him to serious assaults against his sense of mission. He had to be fortified from the beginning with authority of the highest order. Without this word, his anointing would have been incomplete.

Then there is another unexpected development. One might have expected Jesus to move fully into his mission following baptism, empowerment from on high, and the word of divine acceptance, approval, and appointment.

Instead, we read: "And Jesus, full of the Holy Spirit, returned from the Jordan, and was led by the Spirit for forty days in the wilderness, tempted by the devil . . . " (Luke 4:1-2*a*).

Jesus does not rush to population centers to announce the Age of the Kingdom. He remains in the wilderness. I call this a time of suitability testing in which we face the pressures that we will encounter in the work that lies ahead. It is the time in our development to seek clarity about our mission, to determine the appropriate methodology and to discover the system of guidance by which we will go about our work. Although it is a time of pain and struggle, it is nevertheless a very important aspect of the anointing. Some people would overlook this aspect of spiritual growth. They may feel that moments of wilderness wanderings must be the time in which we lose our anointing. But this is not so. The wilderness - the time to find clarity - is an indispensable part of preparation for ministry. What am I to do? What method will I use? Will my method be razzle-dazzle and will it make a big splash now? How will I distinguish the voice of God from the promptings of the adversary? Wrestling to clarify these issues will strengthen us for the struggle to be encountered on the journey.

In Luke's Gospel, the temptation comes to an end "when the devil... departed from him until an opportune time" (Luke 4:13). However, the Matthean account includes a detail that is one of the more comforting dimensions of the anointing: "Then the devil left him, and behold, angels came and ministered to him" (Matthew 4:11).

The "ministry of angels" is heavenly refreshment after such an ordeal. It is the balm of Gilead that soothes the weary traveler along the way. It is release from pain and relaxation of tense muscles. It is an uplift of spirit. It is a ministry of encouragement and congratulations for having endured the assault. It is assurance that all will be well, for the tempter has been forced to retreat for a while. It is a time for recharging for the liberating activity that is about to begin.

And then, at long last, Jesus returned to his home to experience a crowning moment of the anointing. He gave witness to his community of faith that the Spirit of the Lord has anointed him for his vocation of liberation.

Unless a person finds courage to share what his or her pilgrimage has been and what she or he is called to do, the anointing cannot be realized. The power of the community to restrain our freedom in the Spirit can be most intimidating. As Jesus' experience at Nazareth reveals, the anointing will not always be valued by those who have nourished us in faith. To be able to experience the tension between the limited vision of the community of faith and the ever-expanding contours of the kingdom agenda is to discover why the anointing is necessary. The power to be obedient to God's will in the face of human opposition is foundational for prophetic ministry.

James D. G. Dunn in *Jesus and the Spirit,* a comprehensive analysis of the religious and charismatic experience of Jesus and the first Christians, comes to this conclusion: "Jesus believed himself to be the one in whom Isaiah 61:1 found fulfillment; his sense of being inspired was such that he could believe himself to be the end-time prophet of Isaiah 61: he had been anointed with the Spirit of the Lord. Luke is quite justified therefore when he depicts Jesus as opening his public ministry in the full conviction and inspiration of the Spirit upon him" (page 61).

In the light of our discussion, the anointing of the Holy Spirit is that process by which one comes to a fundamental awareness of God's appointment, empowerment, and guidance for the vocation to which we are called as the body of Christ. It is that process that leads us to yield fully to the revealed will of God. Out of a sense of divine power working within us, we are made ready to go forth to be about the task of ministry.

Once again, I list the dimensions of the anointing of the Holy Spirit in the life of Jesus:

1. Jesus had a unique relationship to his heavenly parent. As only begotten Son, conceived by the Holy Spirit, he stands in a class by himself.

2. Jesus was nurtured in his family and the family of faith.

3. Jesus reached the point of vocational readiness to get on with doing that for which he was sent into the world.

4. Jesus acted upon the impulse of the Spirit by obediently following the guidance to submit himself for baptism.

5. Jesus experienced sacramental grace, which comes when one acts in obedience, ie., the baptismal experience.

6. Jesus experienced divine approval, acceptance, and appointment.

7. Jesus experienced power from beyond the self, from on high.

8. Jesus was tested in the wilderness where he was able to come to clarification of mission, methodology, and the system of guidance by which his work would be done.

9. Jesus experienced the ministry of angels.

10. Jesus demonstrated strength to bear witness in his community of faith regarding his spiritual formation for the vocation to which he had been called.

In listing these dimensions of the anointing process, I do not presume precision or some exact formula. The intention is to call attention to specific aspects of Jesus' development so that we can use these insights for enriching our understanding of spiritual formation. A special concern has been to point out that this listing of dimensions of development is broad enough to provide points of identification with the major traditions of nurture and formation. At least at this point in our deliberations, no particular path of spirituality is selected as the preferred route. Following our Lord is the approved route to faithfulness and fulfillment. Can we make that path together toward the fresh anointing of the Holy Spirit?

The call to the church to claim the language of anointing finds support in an excellent study by Professor Gary

M. Burge. In his detailed review of the place of the Spirit in the Johannine Gospel and Epistles, he comes to the conclusion that the hallmark of the Johannine community was the fact that each member was anointed by the Holy Spirit. Thus he entitles his book *The Anointed Community: The Holy Spirit in the Johannine Tradition*. He acknowledges that the occurrence of the term "anointing" is relatively infrequent (I John 2:20, 27), but its significance exceeds the number of times it is mentioned. In commenting on the two verses in I John he says: "In the present texts this anointing forms a part of the overall picture of possession of the Spirit (3:24; 4:13) and divine birthing promised in the Gospel. In John 14: 26, it is promised that the Paraclete 'will teach you all things, and this promise is fulfilled in the anointing described in I John 2:27'" (page 175).

It is only as the members of the community stand in the power of the anointing that they will be able to fulfill their commission. Even as Jesus served in the light of his anointing, so will disciples bear faithful and true witness as that same Spirit indwells believers in community.

The symbolism of the anointing is present in one form or the other in all Christian communities. Consider the following: baptism, confirmation, ordination, the laying on of hands for healing, the consecration and dedication of persons for the work of the church, and even the anointing of emblems and implements within the life of the church - all these in a sense preserve the symbolism of the Divine Presence, bringing power, authority, and grace into the body of baptized believers.

Given the challenges of the secular age, can we continue to talk about our own sense of empowerment and authorization in isolation? The task of calling the church and the age to revitalized spirituality is such that we cannot do it alone. The challenge before the church is to find a way for all of its members to talk together about the anointing of the Spirit and to seek the depth of experience to which it points.

Interestingly, the anointing of the Spirit has not been the specialized language of formation of any particular tradition. Even in the days of Jesus, the anointing of the Spirit was not a popular term to claim. Perhaps the term has been waiting for us to come together to look at what it can mean in a secular age. What promise of revival does it hold for those who no longer experience the sacred in a very vivid way?

My intention is to press for serious exploration of the meaning and the consequence for the church of an openness to the anointing power of the Holy Spirit. What great promise of renewal we would experience if laity and clergy from all denominations could discover new power, new strength, and new courage for the work of the kingdom.

Harry Emerson Fosdick's hymn "God of Grace and God of Glory" expresses well the petition for the anointing proposed here.

> God of grace and God of glory,
> On thy people pour thy power;
> Crown thine ancient Church's story;
> Bring her bud to glorious flower.
> Grant us wisdom, Grant us courage
> For the facing of this hour,
> For the facing of this hour.

THE ANOINTING OF JESUS

George Buttrick's Lyman Beecher Lectures of 1930 were published under the title *Jesus Came Preaching*. The emphasis we have been considering builds upon his title to read "Jesus came preaching under the anointing of the Holy Spirit." As we stand to preach in this name, it would seem reasonable for us to reflect on the conditions and manner of Jesus' example.

We already have given some attention to the nature of Jesus' anointing. Let us turn now to consider the manner of his preaching, which took place under the anointing of the Spirit. After suggesting what may be the general marks of the anointing, more specific attention will be given to the difference it makes in preaching.

Luke's account of Jesus' sermon in the synagogue at Nazareth makes clear that it was a most unusual presentation. Although we have no record of the sermon in its entirety, we may assume that it was very much like the typical synagogal sermon of that period. There was usually the reading of scripture and the exposition of the text along with the other elements of worship - prayer, psalms, and hymns.

But Jesus brought a new quality of presence to the familiar form. His personal identification with the text justifies our saying that he embodied it: "Today this scripture has been fulfilled in your hearing." The hearers not only heard his words, "the eyes of all in the synagogue were fixed on him" (Luke 4:20*b*). There is no doubt that he got their attention and his words actually pricked their hearts. It was impossible for them to remain indifferent. He evoked a response. Preaching under the anointing of the Spirit deeply touches the hearer, evoking either acceptance or rejection of the gospel.

According to Ynvge Brilioth in *A Brief History of Preaching*, the sermon at Nazareth not only serves to bridge between the proclamation in the synagogue and the Christian sermon, but it also provides three basic elements that have characterized preaching through the centuries: *the liturgical, the exegetical, and the prophetic factors* (pages 8-10). With a keen sense of Spirit presence, each of these elements takes on unique meaning. The anointing of the Spirit makes a difference in our understanding of the context, content, and concept of preaching.

Jesus addressed the worshipers at Nazareth in a manner appropriate for persons who had come to yield their lives to the continuing action of the God of Israel. Normally, to worship God is to ascribe highest worth to the divine presence and to open ourselves to the guidance of the Divine Word. All other loyalties are rearranged as God's light breaks forth in the midst of the people. Apparently, his message was too demanding. They were expecting excitement - "what we have heard you did at Capernaum, do here also in your own country" (Luke 4:23*b*). But they were not expecting the coming of a new age or the establishment of a new kingdom. It was not mentioned in the order of worship, nor were the people ready for the exorcism of a narrow nationalism and the adoption of a new agenda on behalf of the poor and oppressed. But when the anointing of the Holy Spirit has taken place, the call to worship is a signal for radical happenings. Such is the liturgical context in which preaching takes place.

The content of Jesus' sermon was taken from the book of the prophet Isaiah. It is not clear whether a lectionary pattern determined the selection of the reading for the day. What seems certain is that Jesus accepts the text from Isaiah as the one that the Spirit chose to bring to new life at that time and place. Comparison of the passage in Isaiah 61 with the verses Jesus is reported to have read in the synagogue suggests that he took the liberty to combine verses or omit phrases. For example, there is no mention of "the day of vengeance of our God" (Isaiah 61:2b). But Jesus did engage in interpretation and dialogue. There is application of ancient text to the contemporary setting. Reference is made to a popular proverb: "Doubtless you will quote to me this proverb, 'Physician, heal yourself.'" Thus, the content is drawn from the sacred texts as well as from the lives and times of the hearers. In addition, the preacher's experiences and insights are offered for the Spirit's use in the preaching moment. Jesus was functioning as an exegete.

When Jesus proclaimed, "Today this scripture has been fulfilled in your hearing," he linked the Christian sermon to the *prophetic tradition*. Brilioth comments on the prophetic feature of the Nazareth presentation:

> The sermon was prophetic in the deepest sense, inasmuch as it is the essential nature of prophecy to speak to the present with divine authority and to transform the historical revelation into a contemporaneous, dynamic reality....Jesus' words have thus given the highest authorization to the claim of the Christian preacher that he or she stands in the prophetic succession. (page 10)

This is why preachers of the gospel cannot be content with just making comments on a text or presenting interesting stories with a religious point of view. A broader concept of preaching is required - one that expects that the God of creation will be present to transform spoken words into deeds of liberation and massive reorientation of life for the sake of the kingdom.

Because of the anointing, Jesus preached with power. He preached not only with words, but his life was the "amen" to the proclamation of his lips. One might wonder whether the disciples were led to believe that they would have a similar experience, enabling them to continue the ministry of announcing the new age. For that matter, to what extent are Christian preachers to expect the power of the anointing to undergird their ministry?

Just as the development of the anointing motif in relationship to Jesus drew primarily from the Gospel of Luke and a reference in Acts of the Apostles, it is important to acknowledge that the language of anointing regarding the early Christians is limited as well. The use of the term, the anointing of the Holy Spirit, in reference to the disciples is found in two major sources. In II Corinthians 1:21-22, Paul says, "Now he which establisheth us with you in Christ and hath anointed us is God, who hath also sealed us and given the earnest of the Spirit in our hearts" (KJV). The other specific references occur in I John 2:20, 27. I John 2:20 says, "But you have been anointed by the Holy One, and you all know." Verse 27 repeats the term: "but the anointing which you received from him abides in you, and you have no need that any one should teach you; as his anointing teaches you about everything, and is true, and is no lie, just as it has taught you, abide in him."

If these are the only specific references, on what grounds do we justify the application of the Holy Spirit anointing to those who preach today? Once we understand the specialized meaning of the anointing during Jesus' time, it becomes clear why it was not generally applied to Jesus, much less to his disciples. Jewish and Roman authorities would be more than mildly suspicious of one who made such claims. Supports of the uniqueness of the claim would be reluctant to apply it to themselves. Hence, any references to the divine empowerment, authorization, and investment, with divine grace for mission must generally be sought under other headings.

There are several terms that refer to such a religious experience: "baptism of/with/in/by the Holy Spirit," "filled with the Holy Spirit," "endued with power," and "Holy Spirit poured out upon us." All these terms speak of the process by which believers are divinely empowered for the work of the kingdom. The anointing may be viewed as just another term in the series of phrases, or it may be broadly conceived so as to include aspects more specifically indicated by the other terms.

The question remains, why lift "the anointing of the Holy Spirit" as the over arching term for empowerment for ministry?

In the first place, the choice of the term "anointing of the Holy Spirit" has to do with the name by which we are called. Acts 11:26 reports: "And in Antioch the disciples were for the first time called Christians." The church at Antioch is an excellent model of the Christian community. It was a church in which the Holy Spirit was a noticeable figure in the unfolding of that community's life. The leaders were "full of the Spirit"; the fellowship was a special training ground for spirit-filled ministry. They sought the mind of the Spirit, they laid hands upon those being sent forth for specific ministries, and they excelled in offering encouragement and sharing resources with those who were in need. It is not surprising that disciples were first called Christians there. It was not necessarily a term of derision as some have suggested. It was quite possibly due to the activity of the Spirit in their midst, which bore remarkable resemblance to Jesus whom they called the Anointed One. In like manner, the lifestyle of that small community showed that they, too, had been anointed by the Holy Spirit. Thus they were not called Jesusians, but Christians - like the Anointed One, they were "anointed ones."

The name by which we are called sets forth the marks by which we are to be known - that is, we are a people, who, like our Lord and through him, have been equipped for a special vocation. With this understanding, the anointing of the Holy Spirit may be viewed as comprehensive, such that various dimensions of the spiritual formation of Christians could be subsumed under it.

On the other hand, there is a more specific use of the term. Highly reflective of Old Testament understanding, the term has come to be associated with the preparation for the performance of a God-given responsibility or the invoking of divine power and presence for deliverance, edification, or sanctification. Baptism, confirmation, ordination, laying on of hands, consecration in the observance of Holy Communion - all preserve the symbolism of the

45

divine presence bringing power, authority, and grace into the human arena.

In the light of these considerations, the anointing of the Holy Spirit is offered as an exhortation to recover the essential meaning of being a Christian and at the same time urges those who would serve the kingdom in specific ways to reconsider the pattern of our Lord's preparation for public ministry. In his anointing, we may have discovered elements of empowerment available to us as we seek not only to bear his name, but to fulfill the mission to which we are invited.

Yet another factor commends the proposal we offer here. It has to do with current developments in the area of spiritual renewal. Pentecostal and Charismatic Christianity has placed the issue of spiritual renewal before the wider church in a very dramatic way. Protestants, Catholics, and Orthodox communions have acknowledged the witness of the movement and in various ways have sought to respond to it as a gift, though other times as a threat. At any rate, the initial phase of interaction has run its course. Most of the central issues are out in the open. Mature participants in dialogue across the various boundaries are aware of the limitations of their positions. They profitably search for ways to spiritual empowerment and for missions which require the unity of the whole body.

The anointing of the Holy Spirit has not been the patented, identifying terminology of any camp of the Christian family. Many of us have used the term but have not built major systems around it. Our various meanings have not served as barriers between us. Therefore, it may be viewed as a term hallowed by our Lord's use of it from the prophecy of Isaiah, commended by its linkage to our name - Christians - and reflective of our contemporary conversations about Holy Spirit renewal. The use of the term may lead us to explore together in a fresh way what it might mean for the whole church to say: "The Spirit of the Lord has anointed us for the work of the kingdom as we face it today."

The proposed use of the term is not intended to serve as another rigid soteriological category with dogmatic insistence that everyone must experience each step according to some predetermined pattern. Rather it is offered as a comprehensive symbol that gathers multiple dimensions of a spiritual growth process experienced by our Lord. I believe that by increasing our awareness of the anointing, we will be called to broader experiences that we may otherwise bypass or ignore. Its virtue is that it combines in concrete ways aspects of spiritual experiences representative of a wide variety of religious traditions. The cutting edge of the proposed model is that it signifies a heightening of awareness of the power and presence of the Holy Spirit as the source of our strength for service. If we share the concept across traditional ecclesiastical boundaries, it will predispose us to take seriously the richness of perspectives other than our own. Thus the ecumenical pursuit of spiritual revitalization draws light from a multiplicity of understandings.

Marks of the Holy Spirit's Anointing

If we are serious about inviting ecumenical consideration, we should be careful to preserve a spirit of openness even as we set about to state as clearly as possible the vision as we have inherited and cultivated it. It is in this spirit that I offer the following preliminary suggestions regarding the marks of the anointing.

Jesus promised the disciples that the power they saw at work in him was available to them as the Holy Spirit came upon them. Pentecost is seen as the fulfillment of the promise, and therefore the disciples came to an awareness of the presence and power of the Spirit.

If we are called Christians, it seems logical that we who are called to serve in Jesus' name ought to have an experience similar to Christ's.

When one claims to be anointed with the Holy Spirit, wholeness should be a noticeable feature. Just as the oil was poured on Aaron's head and went down to the skirts of his garment, so the oil of the Spirit covers all that we are and have. As Christians yielding to the Spirit, our total beings are transformed and no area of life is excluded from the process. Wholehearted dedication and commitment of the collective aspects of our being are in evidence. Just as Jesus was "altogether" what he was in dedication to his mission, the anointing enables us to reflect on his example and respond to his challenge to "love the Lord our God with all your heart, mind, soul, and strength." All of oneself and all areas of one's life are offered to God in fellowship with the community of believers. This is not a new standard of faithfulness. We have always known this requirement of mature discipleship. But the temptation to "nominal" Christian response is ever present. The anointing leads to the mature sense of what a Christian really is —one who integrates the faith in every aspect of life.

The anointed person is *willing to witness* in word and deed to the lordship of Jesus and the kingdom of God. It becomes our vocation to point to God's saving power in the event of the Christ. The anointing of the Spirit is not primarily for our personal edification. It is to enable us to be an embodiment of divine intent. We are anointed to become agents of God who authorizes the process. The anointing is not a ritualistic ceremony to bestow honor; it is an induction into a life-sized role and responsibility. God's plan of redemption requires servants on the earth. In the process of the anointing, selected servants are set forth to function in faith toward the consummation of the great design. Equipped with the anointing, we are prepared to work effectively for God. Even before a task has been fully disclosed, we are held on retainer and stand ready as cherubim poised in flight to be summoned into service.

Faithfulness requires us to be attentive to the guidance of the Spirit. Such a task is impossible if there be *no guidance*. Reliance upon our own judgment is inadequate. The magnitude of the operation and the multiplicity of components that must work together demand divine supervision. Much of what is to be done clearly points in the direction of the coming kingdom. But at times, it will not be obvious how particular assignments fit into the larger plan. This is a special problem in ministry. If we spend too much time wondering whether our work is meaningful, the emotional drain becomes intense. Many drop out because they fail to rely on the guidance system or because there is no sense that they can check in for orders. When we lose a sense of appointment, the inclination is to abandon our post when the assignment seems to be unprofitable and unrewarding. Jesus sustained an awareness of being led by the Spirit by making consistent effort to maintain and renew communication with his Father. This is evident by the long hours he spent in the mountains alone before God. Even gestures such as a sigh, a look toward heaven, point to Jesus' sense of guidance.

The anointing of the Holy Spirit puts into operation a guidance system by which our work for the kingdom is focused and directed. As with faith in general, knowing is not simply the processing of information, but rather living in a unique relationship centered on the being of God. From this point, we learn to act in resonance with the will of God as revealed through a unique relationship. The way we know what to do is not the way of sight, but the way of faith. It is by venturing on faith that verification will come. Sometimes, the way seems quite clear. At other times, it is what pilots call "dead reckoning." It is otherwise called walking in the Spirit. Do not be confused by different terms that may be used. Sense perception, intuition, rationalization, and feelings are all called into action. Abraham leaving Ur of the Chaldees, Paul receiving the call to go over into Macedonia, or Jesus wrestling in the wilderness of temptation or struggling in the Garden of Gethsemane - all these fit in that broad guidance arrangement to which the anointing links us. The outcome is the freedom and courage to act in the confidence that God will bless our efforts. It is the certainty that God will use our faithful action, even if only to teach us how easy it is to confuse signals or how the foolish things of God confound the wise of this world. So from the action that springs forth from the inspired word of knowledge to the desperation move in a crisis situation, we are enrolled in a continuing education laboratory in pneumatological epistemology - a spirit-directed way of knowing.

Furthermore, the anointing of the Holy Spirit results in *power from on high.* The person who is anointed will experience a plus factor as he or she works for the kingdom. This edge is necessary to do the work of God effectively. Jesus said to his disciples, "Without me you can do nothing." It is understandable then why many burn out so soon. They have sought to do a spiritual task without the aid of the Spirit. This is not to deny the significance of human effort. On the contrary, human resources are highly valued and actually enriched by the anointing. The convergence of readiness and divine appointment awakens dimensions of the self that may have been dormant. It is only when the heart signals true readiness that we discover from within a rich reservoir of potentiality. The exhilaration of inner release is part of the feeling of self-transcendence. The sensation of collectedness is sublime as the anointing takes place.

While we use the maturing life of faith as our frame of reference, it is only honest to acknowledge that the emotional experiences of self-transcendence are not limited to the process we are describing. We have witnessed multiple approaches to enlightenment, heightened states of consciousness, psychic tranquility, and various levels of augmented awareness. In terms of the ability to induce such experiences, secular and sacred, humanistic and theistic communities are all colleagues. Of course, they function with different rationales and methodologies and ends. So while we acknowledge the human aspect of a "plus factor," it would be important to identify another dimension of empowerment. Otherwise, our faith claim would be irrelevant. Whatever that other element is, it must be more than the satisfying sensation of inner release.

Once again, we return to Jesus for an identifying mark of power from on high. We don't get much of a sense of Jesus' inner emotional tone during most points of his life. A few references seem to point to what may be called heightened excitement and spontaneous joyfulness. But these are not primary evidences of the Spirit's empowering presence. Rather, the primary evidence has to do with activity in promoting the kingdom with signs and wonders following. The wisdom and knowledge of the human situation and the power to administer the abundant life point to uncommon dimensions of grace. The capacity to encounter principalities and powers, to cast out devils, to heal the sick and raise the dead require some special accounting. And of course, Jesus' resurrection and exaltation speak clearly of a plus factor.

In the light of these considerations, we can identify the plus factor with capacities we have to serve the kingdom or evidence that what we do seems touched or coordinated by a kingdom facilitating agency.

This brings us to another mark of the anointing. Those who testify to the anointing of the Holy Spirit will go forth in ministry fully convinced that their efforts will make a difference. Therefore, the "anointed ones" remain alert and expectant of emerging signs of the kingdom. Just as Jesus gave a summary of kingdom occurrences as authenticating evidence of his vocation, so Christians in whom the Spirit works are to expect signs following.

This expectation doesn't preclude defeats or setbacks. Indeed, there is recognition that kingdom commitment ushers us into areas of conflict. Principalities and powers are waiting to test mortals who press their claim for the sake of the kingdom. Nevertheless, the anointing introduces a new dimension into the conflictual dynamic. No promise has been given that the victory will be celebrated after each encounter. Patience is required as we await the final triumph. In the meantime, the Spirit will vouchsafe accompanying grace to the church.

The anointing of the Holy Spirit transforms these descriptions into living, pulsing reality. How this may happen in a fresh way will be described later. But we should be reminded that effective Christian service is impossible apart from the anointing of the Holy Spirit. Now let us consider why it is unthinkable to preach without the anointing of the Holy Spirit.

PREACHING AND THE
HOLY SPIRIT'S ANOINTING

I have offered my understanding of the anointing and how I see its relationship to new possibilities in the power of the pulpit. I have found others who have made similar connections. I remember finding in my early research a book by Clovis Chappell called *Anointed to Preach*. Although there is not so much an analysis of the anointing process, I did pick up supporting evidence from this great Methodist evangelist that without the anointing, one dare not go forth for the preaching of the word. I also remembered the first book I read that took very seriously the anointing of the Holy Spirit for preaching effectiveness. Though I had seen many books that discussed this subject, I was excited when I learned that James Earl Massey's book, *The Sermon in Perspective: A Study of Communication and Charisma*, was virtually devoted to developing ideas about the anointing.

As Massey suggests in his book, there is first a sense of assertiveness by which to act; second, a sense of being identified with divine will. Next there is a perceived intensity, because what is done relates to the highest frame of reference. Fourth, there is a sense of self-transcendence. Fifth, the kind of instinct for what is done. And sixth, a knowledge that the deed is avowedly moral and religious, in nature and reason; which is to say that the deed is traceable to God's prompting and power, and that it happens for God's own reasons. "The anointed preaching carries the hearers beyond the limited benefit of the preacher's personality and rhetorical abilities" (page 105). It is more than mere enthusiasm. Massey says, "It has to do with mediated meaning and a mediated presence with both affective *and* intellectual levels of life being addressed" (page 106). It is more than communalism. It is a contagion between preacher and people.

Massey's treatment of the topic gives a solid theological base for the further explanation of the role of the anointing in preaching. He distinguishes between a secular understanding of charisma and the biblical/theological meaning of the term. The practical implications that flow from his work are valuable insights into the type of preaching so urgently needed in our time.

But there is yet another definition of the anointing that seems to be in resonance with the approach suggested here. In 1977, Professor Jesse K. Moon, Dean of Southwestern Assemblies of God College, wrote an article ("The Holy Spirit in Preaching") in a denominational publication called *Paraclete* (Fall, 1977, page 27). In his article Moon offers the following definition of anointing. (There is one major difference in the way he views the anointing and the way I try to speak of it.) He says, "The anointing is the special presence of the Holy Spirit in the life and ministry of God's servant, which produces an inspiring awareness of the divine presence. His [and I add *her*] entire faculties are enhanced" and he enumerates: "heightened illumination, courage, wisdom, discernment, faith, guidance, memory, vocation, emotions, intellect, and physical performance." What a list! He says that in the anointing our faculties are enhanced beyond natural abilities. The word of God is quickened to accomplish its regenerating, healing, edifying, and sanctifying objectives. And those ministered to are invested with a God-consciousness, a spiritual enlivening, and an interest in acceptance of the response to the life and ministry of the Anointed One. What a comprehensive listing!

How would you like to have an experience, a series of dimensions of development that made this definition operative in your life? Wouldn't that be something?

Wouldn't the church be on the verge of an extraordinary breakthrough? Well, brothers and sisters, whether it is with respect to Clovis Chappell's understanding, Dean Moon's understanding, or my friend Massey's understanding, I believe firmly that we could be on the threshold of a new way of working together for the appropriation of the power of God for our time if indeed we could find our way nigh unto the pattern of formation that was present in Jesus the Christ.

In workshops, I often ask people to look at the list of the dimensions of the anointing. I ask them to think through which ones they already have experienced and whether there is a desire for these additional dimensions. Quite often, I will stop at this point and have a little prayer meeting, and have the people to ask each other, "What dimensions of the anointing do you find most significantly lacking in your life and which ones do you find already achieved or experienced in your life?" I have them exchange conversations with one another, and then I ask them to pray for one another. The prayers become an extraordinary leveling, for no one is able to say honestly that he or she is more spirit-filled than another. No, each of us prays for the other, because Jesus' standard is exceedingly high, and the grade point average for most of us is not usually all that impressive by comparison.

WHAT DO WE MEAN BY PREACHING?

Let me say something about the concept of preaching which, I think, gets broadened by the anointing.

In the introductory classes I have taught at Union Seminary, we have followed this little tradition: Rather than defining what preaching is, I try to achieve a corporate sense of what preaching is supposed to be. I ask my students to read the major books listed on the course bibliography and then we break up into small groups and each group decides which definition it considers most important. All of the groups report their decisions and we try to prepare a comprehensive definition that the class will agree to adhere to throughout the semester. It has been my delight over the years to preside over a lengthening committee definition of what preaching is.

Here is an example of a working definition:

Preaching is an event in which the living word of God is proclaimed in the power of the Holy Spirit. It is done by a member or members of the covenant community. It is by that process that the preacher serves to focus the dialogue between God and the people in the context of worship. And in that context of preaching, the transforming power of the truth of the gospel is addressed to the concrete realities of day-to-day existence, as well as the issues of eternal significance. It offers an invitation to enter the family of faith, and also calls to maturity and faithfulness those who have committed their lives to the lordship of Jesus the Christ. In addition, preaching is a dynamic, divine-human interaction in which the people of God are nourished for the journey of life, and are challenged and empowered to serve and to celebrate the present and coming kingdom of God.

While this would seem to be an adequate definition, there is something more to say about preaching under the anointing. In my next class, I'll offer this amendment: "Preaching is bearing witness to the resurrecting power of God, which extends itself into the regions of death, so that the new life in Christ breaks forth in all dimensions of the created order." Now that is a strong enough definition to contain what anointed preachers want to be about. This definition means that we are able to have a concept of preaching that demands that the anointing take place.

There are certain understandings of preaching that do not require much of a sense of the anointing. But I am interested in developing a comprehensive concept so that it is understood that in order truly to preach we have to have a full anointing. And not just the first anointing, but a continuing jubilee of reinvestiture, reaffirmation, and covenanting is needed to accomplish Spirit-filled preaching on a continuing basis.

It is critical for us to discuss anointing because there is a necessity for people to have a broader concept of preaching than they have held traditionally. I am convinced that the nature of our culture cries out for more than mere discourse on religious subjects. Preaching about living a Christian existence in our time requires more than a literary gem, which causes people to say, "Ah, she certainly keeps up with the bestseller list." It requires more than a masterful rhetorical style or even a bombastic Pentecostal preaching style.

When I talk about anointed preaching, I am reminded of Ezekiel 37. This text certainly offers a good understanding of what anointed preaching is like.

> The hand of the Lord was upon me, and he brought me out by the Spirit of the Lord, and set me down in the midst of the valley; it was full of bones.
>
> And he led me round among them; and behold, there were very many upon the valley; and lo, they were very dry.
>
> And he said to me, "Son of man, can these bones live?" And I answered, "O Lord God, thou knowest."
>
> Again he said to me, "Prophesy to these bones, and say to them, O dry bones, hear the word of the Lord.
>
> Thus says the Lord God to these bones: Behold, I will cause breath to enter you, and you shall live.
>
> And I will lay sinews upon you, and will cause flesh to come upon you, and cover you with skin, and put breath in you, and you shall live; and you shall know that I am the Lord."
>
> So I prophesied as I was commanded; and as I prophesied, there was a noise, and behold, a rattling, and the bones came together, bone to its bone.
>
> And as I looked, there were sinews on them, and flesh had come upon them, and skin had covered them; but there was no breath in them.
>
> Then he said to me, "Prophesy to the breath, prophesy, son of man, and say to the breath, Thus says the Lord God: Come from the four winds, O breath, and breathe upon these slain, that they may live."
>
> So I prophesied as he commanded me, and the

breath came into them, and they lived, and stood upon their feet, an exceedingly great host.

This passage became real for me as a model of ministry many years ago when Nathan Dell, a Presbyterian minister from Richmond, Virginia, shared with me an exegesis on Ezekiel in Walter Eichrodt's commentary on Ezekiel. When I saw it, I said, "Reverend Dell, the Lord has given you this book in order that you might pass it on to me."

From my own exegesis of the text, I came to a new understanding of my ministry. It made it necessary for me to include in my definition of preaching the concept of the anointing. I call this special ministry the "ministry of raising the dead." It is impossible to operate in this special ministry without the anointing. Here is how I came to that understanding.

As a young Pentecostal minister in Richmond, Virginia, one of my parishioners called me and said, "Pastor, hurry up. My husband is dying, I think."

I rushed over to her apartment, went upstairs where her husband was lying and touched his cold extremities. His eyes were set. There was no sign of breathing. I felt for a pulse, but there was none.

Immediately, I stepped away from the bed and said to the woman, "Yes, I think he's dead."

She looked at me with fixed eyes and said, "Don't just stand there, Pastor, do something."

I was under judgment. I felt my training had not prepared me for this. But in a way, my training did help, for I had done an exegesis on a Matthean passage in which Jesus had sent the disciples out with these instructions: "And preach as you go, saying, 'The kingdom of heaven is at hand. Heal the sick, raise the dead, cleanse lepers, cast out demons'" (Matt. 10:7-8a). The *Interpreter's Bible* said the part about raising the dead was possibly, though not probably, a gloss. So that relieved me somewhat.

But her eyes were fastened on me and would not let me go. That day, I reached a point of reckoning. Even today, when I recall that event, I realize as a minister of the gospel, part of my work is not to flee from the midst of death, no matter what form it may take. For there is death also in separation from God. "Dead in trespasses and sin," is the language that Paul uses. This kind of death often has to do with conditions where there is no longer vitality and therefore there is death. Let me tell you about a time when I got a better understanding of what death ought to mean - a time when I remembered that parishioner in Richmond.

It was at Medical College of Virginia, where I was doing my pastoral clinical education in 1968. I remember they were doing heart transplants at Richmond Medical College. And as pastors, those of us who were in clinical education talked with the surgeons about the ethics of heart transplant operations. We asked the doctor, "How can you know when a person is ready to be a donor?" (Or to put it plainly, we were asking if the one who donates the heart is actually dead.) Whereupon, the surgeon replied, "I leave it up to you theologians to answer questions of the metaphysical meaning of death. In this context, most of what we do is based upon clinical definitions." "Well, then", we asked, "clinically, what do you mean?" He then offered a definition that made me think back on my experience in Virginia. He said, "When there is an examination of the vital signs and we come to the point with a particular patient where there is no longer any prospect for meaningful, purposeful, human existence, based on certain clinical tests, then we are able to declare that patient clinically dead. There may still be life in some sense, but the clinical definition we employ allows us to make use of that patient's heart."

Later, I went back to that parishioner in Richmond and told her the story. I said if that's what death is, a situation where there is no longer any prospect for meaningful, purposeful human existence, well, I've been involved in ministry to the dead for a good while. For every child with leukemia and a bleak prognosis, there is a question about the prospects for meaningful, purposeful, human experience.

In marital relationships where couples have tried and tried, and the desire to try has gone, there is a low prospect for life. In communities where minorities have sought to affirm their own self-interest, their own self-image and self-determination; and secular powers have successfully drained the strength of minorities to be about self-determination - situations of death exist. In my own nation, where, for my protection, I consent to my nation's policy to engage in the death of other people in order to protect me and my ideology: there is a situation of death. Indeed, I had been involved in ministry to the dead for a long time.

As ministers, we must face death with our parishioners and, through the power of the anointing, be a catalyst for the One who conquers all death. To do otherwise ignores the major problems of our time. As I noted earlier, Pannenberg has said the "death of God" is about the nature of the culture; the death of our capacity to experience the sacred; the death of our capacity to have vivid and living experiences of the transcendent. Something has died in our country. Something has died in our western civilization. Something has died which, if it is not recovered, resuscitated, and revitalized, will bring to an end all that our religious traditions have been built upon. We suffer the responsibility of maintaining moral and ethical systems, and definitions of humanizing relationships and patterns of social, economic, and political equality, without the implied sense of the God to whom we are accountable. Something has died, and we keep trying to ask, "Why is our nation becoming mean-spirited, and why are we in the time of bad habits of the heart?"

Why is it we don't seem to understand that we cannot build our country's future on exploitation, discrimination, and imperialistic intrusions in the lives of others? Is it the result of utilitarian or expressionistic individualism? We must calculate and understand how our national programs are intricately linked to the humanizing possibilities of freedom and democracy and hope for all humankind.

Preachers who have not been anointed cannot cope with the death of these times - and there are different kinds of death. We all have a job, a job that cannot be done with just a cute homily, with three points and a poem. Our task is going to take more than that!

I call Ezekiel's ministry an early indication of what

anointed ministry is like. He was called to a ministry of helping those who were in exile experience a sense of the land. Anointed and called to preach to people who had been broken and made dead, separated from their cultic center - anointed and called to give them hope in the midst of their hopelessness. And then after being called, Ezekiel was led through the valley of dry bones. And after being guided, he saw visions and heard the voice of the Lord.

Sons and daughters of the Most High, the Spirit asks, "Can these bones live?" And the immediate answer is, "Oh Lord God, thou knowest." When I look at the reality of our time, the tragic acknowledgment is that anyone who does serious social, economic, political, and spiritual critique in our churches, as well as in our nation, and asks the question, "Can these bones live?"; no matter how great our intellect, how much we think we know, the only honest answer is, "Lord, we do not know what it will take to humanize our cities again. Lord, we do not know what it will take to put back the upward looking and the light and the music back in the hearts of our people. We do not know what it will take to extricate this country from the grips of racism and oppression. We do not know what it will take to influence other countries to live out justice and equality and embrace the vision of human possibilities. We do not know what it will take to awaken in Christianity prophetic judgment against dehumanizing systems, and restore the vision of justice and righteousness in the culture in which we live."

Acknowledging that we know not is one step toward achieving an anointed ministry. If you think you truly understand the situation, you aren't dealing with the real problem. The problem is deeper than immediate knowing. It is deeper than some formula plucked from tradition. Anointed ministry acknowledges we do not know, but nevertheless goes on to take instructions and is reliant on a higher source.

To preach under the anointing of the Holy Spirit is to preach, recognizing, "Lord, I don't know what to say unless you tell me what to say. If you don't tell me, I can do a little exegesis, and I can say some words. But if you don't speak to me, I will not know." Then God says, "Since you don't know, perhaps you are willing to do something that may seem unusual to you."

"Like what, Lord?"

"Prophesy to the bones."

"To the bones? Well, since I don't know, and since you say to do so: O-o-h, dry bones! Hear the word of the Lord."

Then I hear the Spirit say, "If you don't know, just say what I tell you to say. Prophesy deliverance, if you don't know. If you don't know, prophesy hope. You will not have to concoct my message yourself. It will not be like the thesis you struggled so hard to put together. Just say what I tell you to say. There will be those who think you are foolish. There will be times when an examination by the medical profession might conclude you have gone off the deep end ... for prophesying to dead bones could be problematic in a psychological evaluation, but prophesy anyway. Prophesy to the bones."

Consider Ezekiel, who had wisdom born of ignorance acknowledged before God, and who said what the Lord told him to say. This speaks to the content of what we preach. The content, then, is to say what the Lord tells us to say. But more than "content" and words happen when you are going about the ministry of raising the dead, when you are anointed. Because God did use Ezekiel to make things move. There was a noise and a shaking, and the bones came together - sinew, flesh, skin - but no breath in them. And then came this audacious invitation: "Next time, prophesy - prophesy - and if you thought it was foolish for you to prophesy to bones, what I am about to tell you to do is even worse. For at least there is a concreteness within your culture that you can deal with if you see the bones. But now, I want you to prophesy to the wind - the wind - the ruah - the breath - to the Spirit - prophesy."

"But Lord, I can't see it, and I can't touch it, and I cannot quantify it according to laboratory requirements. I have no way of demonstrating it's out there."

That's all right. Prophesy to the wind. The four winds - east and west, north and south. Call to the Spirit that was at work at the dawn of creation, the Spirit that hovered over the mighty deep. Call that same Spirit. The Spirit that was there when there was neither a "then," nor a "there" nor a "when" nor a "where." That same Spirit that God had moving out of God's being on the mighty deep. Call that same Spirit to prevail in the midst of this death. And the preacher called that Spirit.

"O-o-h, four winds. Breathe on our cities (and communities), decaying. Breathe on Harlem. Breathe on New Haven, breathe on our country, breathe on Nicaragua, Soweto, Johannesburg, and Pretoria. Breathe on Afghanistan, Poland, and the Philippines. Breathe on Haiti. Breathe. Four winds, blow upon these slain."

And according to the text, there was a movement because the Spirit had put into the mouth of the anointed preacher the invitation to call the Spirit. It is almost as if part of what lets the Spirit come is someone in the midst of the dead who dares to cry out. It is as if the Spirit cannot stand to remain in its invisibility and its hiding, but must be manifested. When the anointed preacher, invited to stand, therefore cries out, the Spirit hastens to work on his or her behalf.

This yielding process typifies anointed preaching. One has the audacity to respond to the invitation. But if we are afraid of the Spirit; scared because we don't like somebody else's definition; afraid because we are in a culture where spiritual realities are not tangible enough to make sense to talk about; fearful that talking about the Spirit will require some growth in discipline, growth in dedication, growth in yieldedness; afraid that talking about the Spirit will take the organization out of our hands; afraid that the wind of the Spirit will blow in directions we have not considered; afraid to talk; afraid to be open; afraid to preach; afraid to let the Spirit be at the heart of our ministry: then we cannot participate in the ministry of raising the dead, for we are scared of the power by which it shall come. While it is natural at first to experience some degree of fear, we should remind ourselves that love casts out fear - and then remind ourselves that even beyond our fear, is the mysterium tremendum, that holy other that we cannot grasp for ourselves, yet stands with us. When we understand that the fear is reasonable, but that faith is given by grace, we can speak out anyway.

It is time for preachers to seize this moment, which is pregnant with possibilities. We must preach and not be afraid of the Spirit. It is time to move with the fear and acknowledge it, and time to move forward even with the fear that maybe there is no Spirit. Or maybe worse, afraid that there is a Spirit that will bind us to our calling. Until we move beyond our fear of the Spirit's engagement of the centers of our lives and communities, we will not be about the ministry of raising the dead.

With respect to content, we speak what God says. In Ezekiel's case, God is very specific. If we read further than the description of the vision, we will discover that God has more to say. Before God gives a theological statement about the good news of hope, God gives the prophet the sense of the despair of the people. God's Spirit says, "Behold, these bones, the whole house of Israel, says, 'Our bones are dry, our hope is lost, we are clean cut off.'" To be anointed preachers is to understand and for us to listen to the people in our culture and in our world. We must listen to the black folk, the white folk, the poor folk, the rich folk. We need to know what marginal folk are saying, what corporate rulers are saying. To preach requires divine discernment of what all of these people are saying. You can't preach if you don't know what the folks are saying, not only with their mouths, but with the conditions of their lives.

Sometimes the power of the people to deceive themselves is great. And certain cultures have the capacity to mystify, so that the people don't even know what they are saying with their lives; or they learn to say certain things with their mouths to cover up or justify what their lives are saying.

Part of the sermon preparation process is that you have to know what the Lord is saying to YOU about what the people are saying. Then you can hear what God has to say, and that always is a word of hope as well as judgment. The power of the anointed preacher is to be able to hear the word of God, and to know that that word is the word that brings life in the midst of death. My prayer in this discussion is that somebody will decide, "Lord, if that's the ministry to which you are calling me, I dare not go without your anointing."

Let us pray: "Thank you, Lord, for a context in which we can talk about the ministry to which we are called. Thank you for a situation in which we can be open to the possibility that ministry requires a dedication hard to come by. Transform the words we say and the thoughts we share into energy for transformation. And grant that whoever among us has reached the point of vocational readiness will find our time together to be a time of divine confirmation, a time of divine empowerment for the work to which you call us.

"Anoint us afresh and we will serve you aright.

"Through Jesus Christ our Anointed Lord we pray. Amen."

SERMON PREPARATION
AND PREACHING

When I became the professor of preaching at Union Seminary, I decided to secure the services of a preaching coach for the enrichment of my skills as a teacher and preacher. Professionals who teach others need to be taught themselves. It is easy to fall prey to the notion that one has found the final form of excellence. Such an assumption clearly is the beginning of the decline in vitality of any art. It is most certainly the case with preaching where freshness of approach is sustained by the constant quest for the "more excellent way." I personally have benefited from the regular critique, challenge, and encouragement of other skilled communicators.

An occasion to team-teach a preaching workshop for Auburn Seminary led me to J. Philip Swander, the person who was to become my coach for several years. He had been one of my speech teachers when I was a student at Union during the late '50s.

I recall that when Barbara Wheeler, president of Auburn Seminary, convened Phil and me to plan our workshop, I sensed right away that the intervening years had brought Phil insights about preaching that were quite different from what I had learned in seminary. The planning sessions were filled with clashing views and competing perspectives. There was even a point when I considered withdrawing from the contract. Barbara, however, skillfully helped us move beyond our differences and we were able to work through what turned out to be quite an impressive workshop design.

During my work with Phil, I became convinced that he was on to something that could make a positive difference in my preaching and bring a fresh contribution to the teaching of this art. Following the course, I asked him if he would be willing to coach me in the Swander method. He claimed not to have such a method, but consented to work with me if I was interested in breaking out of habits that hinder effective oral communication.

We established regular sessions for a wide range of sermon development exercises. One session would focus on reading the text, another on how to proceed from the text, another on how to identify the sermonic idea. We gave considerable attention to determining the type of exegesis that would be most helpful, while some sessions were spent primarily on aspects of scripting - how to write sermons where the action is as important as the words to be spoken. Still, at other times, work was centered on delivery.

Even though I enjoyed positive response to my preaching, Phil helped me identify areas in which significant change was needed if I were to become a more effective preacher. After extensive work, Phil would accompany me on preaching missions. The feedback from such presentations in the living laboratory would become the focus of subsequent coaching sessions.

I later tested Phil's approach in my own homiletics classes. Convinced of its timeliness and the contribution it would make to the contemporary pulpit, I planned to join Phil in developing a new method in teaching the art of preaching.

Illness, which led to Phil's death in November, 1986, interrupted our collaborative efforts. But my deep and abiding gratitude for his contribution to my development required public acknowledgment.

The Lyman Beecher Lectures at Yale was one of the last preaching events Phil attended with me. I had asked him to come along to give greetings. Though weakened by his illness, Phil came and his participation provided a very important dimension of what I wish to say about how the anointing makes the difference in preparation and delivery of sermons.

He prefaced his remarks by saying that when he was invited, "I had the feeling from somewhere that I shouldn't just [come and say] hello, but that I should share with you." Then he read these words of Paul recorded in Romans 8:11-27:

> If the Spirit of him who raised Jesus from the dead dwells in you, he who raised Christ Jesus from the dead will give life to your mortal bodies also through his Spirit which dwells in you.
>
> So then, brethren [and sisters], we are debtors, not to the flesh - for if you live according to the flesh you will die, but if by the Spirit you put to death the deeds of the body you will live. For all who are led by the Spirit of God are children of God. For you did not receive the spirit of slavery to fall back into fear, but you have received the spirit of sonship [and daughterhood]. When we cry, "Abba! Father!" it is the Spirit ... bearing witness with our spirit that we are children of God, and if children, then heirs, heirs of God and fellow heirs with Christ, provided we suffer with him in order that we may also be glorified with him.
>
> I consider that the sufferings of this present time are not worth comparing with the glory that is to be revealed to us. For the creation waits with eager longing for the revealing of the sons [and daughters] of God; for the creation was subjected to futility, not of its own will but by the will of him who subjected it in hope; because the creation itself will be set free from its bondage to decay and obtain the glorious liberty of the children of God. We know that the whole creation has been groaning in travail together until now; and not only the creation, but we ourselves, who have the first fruits of the Spirit, groan inwardly as we wait for adoption as sons [and daughters], the redemption of our bodies. For in this hope we were saved. Now hope that is seen is not hope.

For who hopes for what he or she sees? But if we hope for what we do not see, we wait for it with patience.

Likewise the Spirit helps us in our weakness; for we do not know how to pray as we ought, but the Spirit itself intercedes for for us with sighs too deep for words. And he who searches the hearts of [human beings] knows what is the mind of the Spirit, because the Spirit intercedes for the saints according to the will of God.

When Phil said he had "the feeling from somewhere" that he shouldn't simply say hello, but should share this passage, he was expressing an awareness that the anointing of the Spirit brings. Phil didn't speak easily about the Holy Spirit in that way. Indeed, he was uncomfortable with glib claims of spiritual unctions. But his comment about a "feeling from somewhere" was accompanied by an upward tilt of his head - the unspoken must be taken very seriously, he always insisted. And those who heard him read the text could bear witness that he communicated a powerful sense of "something within" as he read the passage in which Paul describes the work of the Spirit.

Without doubt, Phil had prepared for the reading of the text, making use of all his insight about oral reading. He taught that preparation of a sermon included serious effort at effective reading of the scripture. A preacher who doesn't respect the word enough to strive for excellence in leading the congregation to hear it doesn't deserve the opportunity to present his or her manuscript as if such words are somehow more important than the Bible.

Moreover, Phil's presentation gave evidence that he was prepared and acquainted with that about which he was reading due to an intimate relationship with the Spirit. Through months of battling with his illness, he had entered a new depth of Spirit awareness. In his own suffering, he had begun to experience a glory and companionship of the Spirit he had not talked about before. With increasing explicitness, Phil had started to share how he was experiencing the Spirit as a source of strength. I would be reluctant to make these comments about my dear friend were it not for the overwhelming corroborating evidence reflected in his reading that night in Marchand Chapel at Yale.

When I review the presentation on videotape, I get a renewed sense of how important it is for preachers to prepare by entering into a knowing relationship with the Spirit about which we speak. Thus a first principle of preparation has to do with experiencing a firsthand ministry of the one who sends the word. Even before we plunge into exercises designed to give technical competencies, we as preachers should open ourselves to the ministry of the Holy Spirit. This is foundational for the preparation of every sermon.

Nearly a decade before Phil's memorable reading of Romans 8, I had written a sermon from the same text on how the Spirit sustains our hope. I return now to those words to describe how the Spirit helps to prepare the preacher for the ministry of the word. I believe the anointing of the Holy Spirit helps the preacher to understand the living spiritual encounters that Paul describes in Romans 8: "If the Spirit of him who raised Jesus from the dead dwells in you, he who raised Christ Jesus from the dead will give life to your mortal bodies also through his Spirit which dwells in you" (verse 11). Life in the Spirit is the special provision for the Christian by which we are renewed in hope.

The presence of the Spirit will make the difference between our failure and our fulfillment. It was so in the case of Jesus. The Spirit of God snatched the victory from death and the grave and established a firm foundation of hope for the whole creation. If there is to be a victory march at the end it will be through the work of the Holy Spirit.

The link between the work of the Spirit and the Christian's hope is interestingly reflected in the movement of the writings of Jurgen Moltmann. His book *Theology of Hope* gave widespread contemporary expression to the hope motif in Christian theology. Later he gave attention to the reality and centrality of the cross in salvation history in his book *The Crucified God*. But it seemed almost inevitable if he wanted to promote hope that he would have to write another volume emphasizing the Holy Spirit. This he did in *The Church in the Power of the Spirit.*

Once again, Romans 8 has anticipated theological and existential necessity. So central is the Spirit in Paul's understanding of the Christian pilgrimage that he says in the ninth verse, "Any one who does not have the Spirit of Christ does not belong to him." The point of the statement is not to exclude. Rather, the intent is to make clear the basis of inclusion.

Beyond this general statement of the importance of the Spirit, Paul goes on to give some concrete ways in which the Spirit works to help fulfill our hopes. In so doing, he shows special pastoral sensitivity. Those being encouraged to stake their lives on the power and faithfulness of the Spirit would wish for some definite experience to undergird their commitment and trust. It seems there should be some definite way we can experience such power, at least in an anticipatory way. There ought to be some hint in the here and now of that power on which we will rely when death holds us in its grip. If that power cannot lift us above despair, it will be difficult to believe in its power to lift us beyond death. If there is no power to cope with temporal frustrations, whence the force to deal with the eternal negation of death?

Earlier we quoted the negative part of verse 15, but now let us hear the whole verse along with verses 16 and 17. Here we find one of our first insights regarding what the Spirit does to move us toward hope.

> For you did not receive the spirit of slavery to fall back into fear, but you have received the spirit of sonship. When we cry, "Abba! Father!" it is the Spirit himself bearing witness with our spirit that we are children of God, and if children, then heirs, heirs of God and fellow heirs with Christ, provided we suffer with him in order that we may also be glorified with him.

What is offered here is not the concept of adoption, but rather the experience of adoption. It is in the midst of a mood of abandonment that we are surprised by sounds coming from a deep place within. The sounds express confidence that "this is my Father's world and I am his child." Or, "I was feeling like a motherless child, but now I feel the tenderness of Mother's love." Such sentiments are not the logical conclusions to an orderly thought process. In fact, the argument had seemed to be going in the other direction. But out of nowhere there is an about-face and then the cry, "My God, my God." How does this happen? It is the Spirit making us remember that Jesus Christ is our elder brother and that the legacy of "glory beyond suffering" belongs to us also. It is this power that calls forth "spirituals" from slaves with chains on their ankles. When the Spirit works like this, hope becomes a real option again. But there's more. The scripture says the "Spirit helps us in our weakness, for we do not know how to pray as we ought."

This is what Paul had experienced so many times - not the Spirit as a principle of divine activity in human history, but as a very present help in the time of weakness. When the complications of internal conflict robbed him of the right words to pray, the Spirit came to his aid, bypassing his impasses and blending his sighs and groans with the persisting will of God. This freed him to be where he was, with all his doubts and fears, and at the same time kept him open to the invitation to follow the promise to the end.

I have felt the power of the Holy Spirit as a helper in my own prayer life. I remember once when I couldn't find the words to appropriately address the God of my life. I knelt at my bed, stretched forth my arms and moved my shoulders in writhing jerks of anguish. All I could utter were sighs and groans. But afterwards, I felt so much better that I said, "Perhaps I can pray now." But it seemed the Spirit said to me, "You don't need to pray any more now. Heaven is equipped to receive choreographed prayer. Also, your sighs and groans have already been decoded and help is on the way."

Your experiences may not have been like mine, but I believe we all have experienced the Spirit as our help. Perhaps it was by giving us a little more strength when a task seemed more than a match. Or it may have been in a struggle for justice when everyone seemed against you and the Spirit helped you endure the isolation. How powerfully Martin Luther King, Jr., witnessed to this kind of help in the midst of his times of stress and strain!

Paul Tillich preached a sermon on spiritual presence in which he enumerated some of the varied manifestations of the Spirit's help:

> The Spirit can work in you with a soft but insistent voice, telling you that your life is empty and meaningless, but that there are chances of a new life waiting before the door of your inner self to fill its void and to conquer its dullness. The Spirit can work in you, awakening the desire to strive toward the sublime over against the profanity of the average day. The Spirit can give you the courage which says "yes" to life in spite of the destructiveness you have experienced around you and within you.

Each person knows his or her own particular experience of how the Spirit has nourished hope. What we share is the question of how we would have survived without those timely interventions. How important for each of us to know that such help is the normal provision for those whose hope is in the power of the resurrected Lord!

There is yet another way by which the Spirit gives us the courage to hope. I call it the experience of eschatological epistemology. The mysterious power and weight of this particular experience constitutes a new kind of knowledge that can only be understood from the vantage point of those who believe that the world as we know it must come to an end. Paul boldly asserts this claim in verse 28, saying, "We know that in everything God works for good with those who love him, who are called according to his purpose."

How can we say "we know" even before the end has come? Things are very much in process, and sometimes our hopes seem to be in the middle of an aborted process. How can we say "we know"? We can say it only because the Spirit, who communicates with us and helps us, seems to know what we do not know, can see what we cannot see. The Spirit sees the future depth implanted in the past and present. The Spirit's relationship to the future exceeds our comprehension. The Spirit has a way of convincing us that the plan of redemption is working and everything will come out all right and that in every threatening thing and in every comforting thing, the Lord is working to fulfill God's promise about what shall be.

Occasionally, saints are given rare previews of the creation set free from bondage. Paul speaks of such a transcendent experience. Most of us, however, are only privileged to see faint intimations of things to come. It may happen as we share word and sacrament, or as we work and reflect on impossible situations. Although we see through a glass darkly, it is enough to quicken our hope. Love's advance disclosures at least let us know the sufferings of this present time are not to be compared with the glory that shall be revealed. It is a kind of end-time knowing, which we can experience through life in the Spirit.

On the basis of eschatological epistemology, Martin Luther King, Jr., was able to say: "I've been to the mountaintop. And my eyes have seen the coming of the glory of the Lord. I may not get there with you, but I know that we as a people will make it to the promised land." When we talk like that, people will ask us, "How do you know?" We can only reply, "The Spirit tells us so," and having reviewed the promises of the word, our spirits have found the courage to join in singing, "We shall overcome!"

A minister who has experienced the ministry of the Spirit as described above already has a headstart for the preaching of the word.

After stressing the importance of the anointing of the Spirit, someone once responded as if I were suggesting that we can be relieved of the rigor and tedium of sermon preparation. "Oh, I just want to thank you for telling us about the anointing of the Spirit. You know, I have always felt that the hard labor of traditional homiletical rules was more than was necessary.... Thank you for showing us how to preach without all that unnecessary toil."

I usually respond to such comments by finding a tactful

way of declining the gratitude and explaining that I do not believe the anointing of the Holy Spirit relieves us from the responsibility of thoughtful diligence in exchange for magical toil-free preparation. If we need a proof-text, a better choice would be Luke 11:42c: "these you ought to have done, without neglecting the others."

But the anointing of the Spirit undoubtedly assists us and makes the difference in the overall preaching process. We might wonder if, as a result, the preaching will be more lively, or if sermons will become more biblical. We might ask whether such preaching involves more of the preacher's personal experiences, and whether it requires more or less time, or a more or less scholarly approach. There also may be questions about whether the sermon preparation should follow traditional rules of homiletical development. What will the difference be?

One way to respond to these issues is to identify areas of longing regarding improved preaching. We must first identify what it is that we would wish for the strengthening of our preaching. What areas of increased competency would give you personally a greater sense of satisfaction in your moments of proclaiming the good news? What's lacking now? What could be better? Have you had any substantive feedback on your preaching? What intimations of the Spirit have suggested, "Well done, so far, but there is more that can be done"?

Perhaps you desire greater ease in getting to the central idea of the sermon. Do you have trouble finding the illustrations? Would you wish for greater freedom of expression? Do you wish for more depth of analysis, a better sense of timing, or a better structure for your sermon?

I raise these questions because the true anointing will help complete the unfinished dimensions of one's growth process in the preaching of the word. I strongly believe that the anointing of the Holy Spirit can help in very definite ways. When we experience the anointing, we are incorporated into the continuing drama of salvation as it is energized and guided by the Holy Spirit.

In fact, since the anointing is that process by which we

come to a fundamental awareness of God's appointment, empowerment, and guidance for the work of the ministry, there is a kind of continuous flow in the process of the Spirit's unfolding of our mission, and of our gifts, and the focus of our responsibilities. The Spirit carries us so forcefully that the traditional distinctions of preparation of the preacher, preparation of the sermon, preparation for delivery, and the delivery of the sermon itself become subsidiary. What is left is a continuous ebb and flow of movement within the power of the Spirit. First with one dimension of preparation and then another, always moving as the Spirit directs.

In other words, for us to be caught up in the Spirit, we must be open to receive with a heightened intensity whatever the anointing power revealed in Jesus the Christ has for us. Our prayer must be that the people who await our return from the ministers' workshop will anticipate greater power in the pulpit, and therefore there will be more strength in the pew for the work we are called to do.

When I think of the anointing and how it affects our preparation, my mind goes back to Howard Thurman. There are interesting similarities between his and Phil Swander's delivery pace. Thurman would stand, wait, and then close his eyes. He would look up and say something like, "Oh Lord, thou hast searched me and known me." And as he continued, something happened to the audience. They discovered a great interest in the one Thurman was looking toward.

When Thurman read Psalm 139, we began to understand part of the sermon preparation process. It was not so important that we heard or understood all of the words. What was important was that we were moved into a presence. We were enveloped - surrounded by a presence - and what a glorious presence! It was a presence that knows our down-sittings and our up-risings; a presence that understands our thoughts afar off and is acquainted with all our ways.

This presence, as the psalmist notes, was there at our embryonic beginnings, though our existence was not yet visible to the naked eye. It worked with our unformed substance, allowing the process of mitosis to continue - dividing of the cells, so that after the course of time, every member was formed.

And then the psalmist upon whom Thurman helps us to eavesdrop goes on to say, "God was there, helping to make my toes into toes, and my fingers into fingers; my head into a head, and my foot into a foot." That presence was there. And then, this presence followed us all the way. Even when we took the wings of the morning and dwelled in the uttermost parts of the sea, that presence was there. And then, if we made our bed in Sheol, that presence was there too. Even in the conflict with enemies, that presence was there, searching us, lest our hearts be found to have impediments that would block the experience of that presence. Such knowledge is too wonderful for me. It is high. I cannot attain to it.

This is my way of saying that my understanding of the anointing is the *experience of the presence of the Spirit.* You can see we are not talking about anything new. We are talking about a reality in which and with which you have lived, and moved, and had your being since you began. We are talking about a presence that was with you when you thought you had reached the end of your line; the presence that was with you in the confusion and conflict of adolescence; that shepherded you through the uncertain years of early adulthood; a presence that has been with you all the way from then even until now.

Therefore, it is not appropriate for us to talk about the anointing of the Holy Spirit as if what we have to do is come up with some brand-new language, some brand-new experience; as if you have to take a trip to the East to get in touch with it. What we are talking about is something we already know something about, because our knowing has been in the context of that something. What we are talking about does not require us to ask, "Yes, tell us about that. That's a new idea."

No, we can't be like the little boy whose mother wanted him to ask for the molasses correctly. He kept saying, "Mama, I want some 'lasses" and the mother would correct him, saying, "You mean, molasses." He said, "Well, I can't ask for *mo*lasses if I ain't had *no* 'lasses."

If we are concerned about the anointing, it may be useful to pause and have a doxology, giving thanks to God for the work of the Spirit. "God, thank you that when I was not, your Spirit called me into being. Thank you for healing me of all my childhood diseases that could have taken me away but didn't because of your Spirit. Thank you for being with me in my early development even though I didn't know the names of the soteriological categories. Thank you for safeguarding my pilgrimage to this point. And even though I may not be where I ought to be, thank you God, for you have shepherded me all the way; and because you have brought me all the way, I thank you for being invested in how far I've come. I thank you for the assurance of knowing you will never abandon me."

Each of us can say a similar doxology for indeed God *is* with us. It is this understanding that brings us to sermon preparation. For the sermon begins with the experience and understanding that we live in that presence.

There is another dimension of preparation that focuses on the responsibility of proclamation. For in the anointing we become aware of a fundamental truth: the Spirit is *in the process* with which we are involved. How I love these words of Jesus from John 16:12 - given to the disciples as he prepares to go. He says to them: "I have yet many things to say to you, but you cannot bear them now. When the Spirit of truth comes, [the Spirit] will guide you into all the truth; for [the Spirit] will not speak on [the Spirit's] own authority, but whatever [the Spirit] hears, [the Spirit] will speak, and [the Spirit] will declare to you the things that are to come." This speaks to me about the work of the Spirit in the process of getting ready for the sermon. Remember, we are already in the Spirit. Therefore, it is just a matter of the continuation of that experience.

I like to think of the Spirit the way Jesus has characterized it. According to this text, the Spirit becomes a director of continuing education for our spirits. We are not beginners. This is not kindergarten. We are already on the way. But the Spirit that brought us this far continues to direct our paths. So preparing a sermon is not done by ourselves. The director, who has been with us all the way, is standing right there with us. We are not in the ministers' workshop alone. The Spirit is there with us.

Have you ever experienced this collaboration? If you have, you'll know that it is much different from working by yourself. Much of the anxiety and dread associated with the preparation process is removed by this experience of collaboration. It enables us to say, "I'm not here by myself. Somebody is here with me in the process." It is as if the Holy Spirit *is* the preacher; therefore, we are honored to have the opportunity to collaborate with the Spirit in this sacred process. This means all of the heaviness and our questions of "Oh, my goodness, what do I say and how do I do this?" are somehow moderated by our tag-team relationship with the Spirit. And oh, what a joy it is to work with this director of continuing education who is able to take on different roles and supply our every need. The Spirit becomes a tour guide, through time and space, through truth and grace, leading us, so we can see, understand, and proclaim what is happening.

This leading is a kind of exegetical process that pulls together our preparation. This tour guide is the master of terrain of all time and experience and eternity. It is out of this data that the sermonic event will flow. Sometimes we are taken through death valley - Ezekiel will witness to this - to help us see the reality of our times. At other times, our tour guide stops us on the plain of the seemingly uneventful. Nothing appears to be happening. Nothing is going on in this parish. Nothing is going on in the lives of these people. But the guide will say, "You have missed the pain which is etching the deep valleys in the minds of these people. There is something for us to do here."

Our guide, with us in preparing our sermon, takes us to the New Jerusalem and allows us to see a river flowing through the midst of the streets of the city, with trees on either side, with leaves on the trees for the healing of the nation, and a fruit for every month of the year, and to see the foreheads of the people, which shine with the seal of God, and light emanating. (Revelation 22;1-5) And we can see this even from the valley of death or the plain of the uneventful. It is the Spirit. The Spirit that helps us to see what we otherwise would not be able to see. The Spirit identifies events that are too important to be trusted to our unaided vision. For we need this glorious bifocality, through which time and eternity are in our view.

Furthermore, Jesus says to us: "There are many things I have to say to you, but you cannot bear it now" (John 16:12). But when the Spirit comes, the Spirit will discern what you are ready to receive - what the time and the context call for. One cannot arrive at point "B" before mastering point "A." Therefore, the Spirit is likely to tell us what dimension of growth we should be entering at a given point in time. We need not feel anxious about being perfected overnight. The fullness of the anointing is experienced gradually, step by step.

It is all right to develop a single point in time and space. Don't try to preach ten or fifteen different points. One point can give a portal into the heart of eternity from which all the blessings flow. This enables the preacher to focus and get the right word. We also can see that the Spirit becomes a courier of the word that God sends to us. That is, when there *is* a special word. When there is a word that we otherwise would miss, the Spirit, having brought us all the way, is able to stir our hearts and allow us to hear this word. The Spirit also acts as a kind of cosigner of our "epistles of encouragement," by helping us to reach the hearts and minds of the people.

And yet, the Spirit will not lead us unless we put forth our share of the effort. We may be led to go to the library to research a topic. We may be led not to only read that book we were seeking, but to dig deeper. After much searching on our part, the Spirit may help us to find a totally different source that is most valuable to our efforts.

Through this collaborative process, we begin to enjoy preparation. Some of my heightened moments of excitement, which often exceed the excitement I've experienced during the actual preaching, were had during the stage of preparation. Sometimes it is so exciting to have the Spirit guiding me as I prepare to preach that I have to stand up and walk around a little bit because it is so hot, so intense, when the anointing brings the collaborator into the process of "getting the sermon out."

But finally, there's a time when the sermon must be preached. By the aid of the Spirit, the sense becomes apparent that "this is the word that ought to be said."

At this time, the Spirit even helps us to deliver the sermon. In Acts 10, Peter, who already had experienced this visitation on the day of Pentecost, is able to sense what this collaboration is all about. At Cornelius's house, the people experience the presence of the Spirit. As Peter is moved to go to Cornelius's house and begins to preach, he tells the others that he has come to realize God is no respecter of persons and that they must know that in any place where there are those who are the upright and who are listening to the voice of God, God receives them. Peter went on to talk about Jesus and how *he* was anointed. As he preached, something happened that I believe is particular to the moment of the anointing. While Peter was preaching, the same Spirit that brought him to that place and prepared him, also prepared the people. The anointing in the pulpit is by the same Spirit effecting in sense of "bringing about" the anointing in the pews. If it is not happening in the congregation, even if it appears to be happening in the pulpit, it will not be the moment of preaching we anticipate in the power of the Spirit. In this situation, God had been at work within the worshipers at Cornelius's house as well.

It is the task of the Spirit to convene the community of those who are being made ready. It is the work of the Spirit to lead us in the moment of proclamation, to guide us even beyond our own inclination. It is the Spirit at work, enabling preachers to do their part, but at the same time, connecting with what's happening within the listeners.

Peter experienced the outpouring of the power of God in the midst of that community. The authenticity and integrity of that community were powerfully confirmed by the Spirit. The community was strengthened, and Peter was invited to stay so that he could talk about the implications of what had been going on there.

This means the anointing is not just manifested in a

heightened moment of excitement, but it lingers for the teaching moment - to talk about the implications of the experience. A liturgical moment follows as Peter baptizes the people. He engages in a little ecclesiology. "Can we forbid these to be baptized, who have experienced the Spirit even as we have?" (Acts 10). This is the anointing which we must appropriate to develop the quality of our preaching.

If we preach out of the experience of the anointing such as is described in Jesus the Christ, and if we appreciate the nurturing that shapes our very lives, and if we experience the Spirit as a collaborator in the process of normal preparation, we can expect to receive the text and message that is sent by God. Sometimes this is given through the lectionary or by way of the events of the time. It also can be given by the underscoring of meaning in our own lives.

I could have discussed questions often brought up about the exegesis or about word studies. I could have talked about use of reference materials or finding sermon illustrations. Discussion could have been given to structure, whether it be narrative in form, or reveal inductive style. I could have talked about all that. But these dimensions are given within the superintendency of the Spirit. It is most important that we first allow ourselves to enter into the collaboration to achieve fervent and life-transforming preaching.

To be sure, we as preachers must enter a contract with the Spirit. We have to agree to cooperate and allow ourselves to be used by the Spirit. Preachers nourished in the Pentecostal tradition used to sing the song simply entitled "Yes." We must be able to say "yes" to the Spirit - and mean it! "Yes, I'll say what you want me to say. I'll do what you want me to do. Yes, I'll be governed by your power in my daily life as I communicate the word." We even may need to ask the Spirit to help us say yes, to teach us to yield to the leading of the Lord. This is part of what happens when the anointing becomes real for us.

Then once we have contracted with the Spirit, we need to contract with the task. We preachers should individually arrive at the point of determination where each of us

83

can say, "Yes, I'll do it." Too often we struggle because we haven't gotten to this point. It is difficult to be about a ministry of preaching while still being reluctant to do it. Let me be clear on one point. We don't have to *want* to preach. But we should be willing, for there is little rest for the anointed preacher who resists the mandate. As Paul said, "Woe to me if I do not preach the gospel!" (I Corinthians 9:16c).

Once we consent, we are to surrender all we have to the process. Psalm 103 encourages us to bless the Lord with all that there is within us. Even the resources around us should be incorporated in our preaching. We should learn to make use of whatever is present in the setting, as well as work around possible obstacles. It is best to allow time before the event to check details such as lighting, ventilation, and sound. And if we find the atmosphere isn't conducive to the proclamation of the word, we should do what we can to get it in order. I call this aspect of preparation "contracting with the space."

Then we must be sure to contract with ourselves. We must remind ourselves that we have entered into this agreement with the Spirit, knowing that the ways of the Spirit aren't always predictable. This would suggest that we have a need of checking in with the Spirit even before we get started. Are we willing to be fully available to the power of the Spirit in this moment of communication? What if it involves more than verbal expression? Are we willing to lend a hand, a foot? If our low tones are needed, and perhaps our high tones . . . will we yield ourselves? We need to yield our total beings. What if a smile is needed? "You've got it." What about a frown or a nod? "You've got it."

Finally, we must not forget to contract with the people because the event can't take place through the preacher alone. The moment of anointed preaching is a *corporate reality.* So we should elicit from waiting congregations a willingness to respond to the Spirit. How incongruous it is to have a spirited message where only the preacher has contracted. The congregation also has to enter the contract. We must all say, "Lord, yes. Yes to the impulse of your

Spirit. Yes to the guidance in our souls." We must accept the implications for our lives and not fear the visitation of the Lord, trusting God's word that if we be led by the Spirit, everything will be done in order. So, we preachers and our congregations need to be committed and contracted together.

As we grow, we are able to move beyond hindrances to ministry, too, such as preconceived notions about who God would choose to use. We need not be intimidated by the uniqueness of someone else's experience, be they male or female. While we have come a measurable distance, the church still has far to go in this regard. A full appreciation of individuals' various gifts would help us to more fully appropriate the anointing.

For example, I have noticed that women bring from their experience a special knowledge about how to prepare and how to deliver. I was impressed that the texts in Advent kept talking about Mary (Luke 1:57 and Luke 2:7) "bringing forth" and Elizabeth "bringing forth." And as I reflected on their conversation, I was challenged by the observation that they brought to completion that which had been started in them. I recalled the many things I had started, but had not yet "brought forth."

Mary said that which she brought forth was conceived by the Holy Spirit. And of course Elizabeth, who was advanced in age, acknowledged that in her case the Spirit also was to be credited. Both realized that what was at work in them was made possible by the Holy Spirit.

Not only were these two special births made possible by the Spirit, but the Spirit, which conceived, also hovered through the process of gestation. Mary and Elizabeth knew the Spirit was with them, for when Mary went to greet Elizabeth, the Spirit overshadowed both of them and the baby leaped in Elizabeth's womb. Just as it happened for Mary and Elizabeth, the Spirit is with us during various stages of development.

And so it is with sermon development. The Spirit is with us during conception, gestation, and even during the moment of delivery.

This revelation helped me to understand what preaching

under the anointing is like. We must be able to deliver. This requires for us to be willing and to be strong in both mind and body to be able to handle this most sacred responsibility.

Then we have to have the capacity to wait a while. Sometimes, the sermon won't come when we want it to come. We have to learn to wait on the Lord.

We even have to learn to endure pain. In fact, the sign of pain is a good one. Those who avoid pain and struggle will not bring forth life in the pulpit. Indeed, the pain is likely to intensify just before a breakthrough can occur.

Preachers must master techniques of their art. We must learn to bring forth...shallow breathing and deep breathing. We must know when to push and when to relax. Then we must know when to turn loose, let it go and trust that the life-giving Spirit, who stands with us through all of this, can complete the "bringing forth." We don't have to do our preaching alone. In fact, we cannot do it alone.

If only we preachers would allow ourselves to experience more of the anointing. If the churches across the nation and around the world would allow this to happen, the anointing would bring about transformation in our time.

THE SPIRITUAL FORMATION
OF ANOINTED PREACHERS

The world needs anointed preachers, not just because there is some biblical basis to support this idea, but because full response to the will of God is impossible apart from that anointing. It was so in Jesus' time and so it is today.

We all know, from the account given in the fourth chapter of the Gospel according to Luke, that Jesus encountered a world that was almost never ready to receive the acceptable year of the Lord. We realize too that some benefits we enjoy now are so dear to us that we aren't willing to accept God's invitation for a new arrangement. If Jesus hadn't been an anointed preacher, prophet, Son of God, do you think he could have been faithful to his responsibility on the occasion of his first sermon? Luke makes it clear that the enterprise about which Jesus was concerned was always caught up in the conflictual dynamics of one kingdom over another. And the consequences of rocking the boat, or of calling into question the final authority of the earthly kingdom, was a speedy ouster from the congregations of the status quo.

The world today is just like that. If we dare to preach the gospel of the kingdom; dare to make plain the social, economic, and political, as well as the traditionally defined spiritual consequences of pursuing that kingdom, we should expect conflict. If, in addition to making God's truth plain, we show concrete implications of the gospel, we would dare rise up and move programmatically toward dismantling the claims of the dominion of death, dismantling the claims of the earth's kingdom, boldly proclaiming that the reign of God's life has been established in our midst - if we do that, each of us might expect resistance on many fronts.

Only by the anointing of the Spirit does the vision of God's kingdom become so etched in the mind and heart that action must flow from it. Only through anointed preachers will death and its structure of oppression be exposed for what they really are. Then guardians of that dominion can be set free from their self-strangulation and be brought to the fresh air of the wind of the Spirit. Only anointed preaching will make plain the truth, which makes transformation of life possible for both the oppressor and the oppressed.

I am not just talking about stirring up preachers with "hallelujahs." I am not trying simply to urge certain groups to raise the temperature of their preaching, though I admit that would have been my purpose a few years ago.

This discussion attempts to delve deeper than that. Our agenda must be more serious than that if what we have considered in the previous chapters is true. Our ministry must truly be about "raising the dead." Our ministry must be about overthrowing the power of death in all of the forms in which it is manifested. If our nation is to be raised from the dead, and if we are to be raised from the dead, and if our institutions (ecclesiastical, social, and political) are to be raised from the dead, we need anointed preachers of the gospel.

While we realize that God already has broken the dominion of death, we also should recognize that if the good news is not delivered, powers prevail that allow death to prop itself up and indefinitely postpone the glorious liberty of the sons and daughters of light and life. Then, the gospel story, with all of its truth about God's resurrection power, would be dormant. It would be as if the eighth verse of Mark's Gospel account of the Resurrection were the last verse. Without the proclamation of the good news, those added words in the sixteenth chapter, verses nine through twenty, would never have been appended to the Gospel account.

Here is the passage from Mark: "And they went out and fled from the tomb; for trembling and astonishment had come upon them; and they said nothing to anyone, for they were afraid."

Think about that. This could happen in pulpits all across the nation. "They said nothing, for they were afraid." God forbid.

As we read these verses in the Revised Standard Version, we notice several blank lines separating verses eight and nine. This indicates that the verses which follow may have been a later addition. But an anointed reading takes seriously even the spaces between the lines.

Now when he rose early on the first day of the week, he appeared first to Mary Magdalene, from whom he had cast out seven demons. She went and told those who had been with him, as they mourned and wept. But when they heard that he was alive and had been seen by her, they would not belive it.

After this he appeared in another form to two of them, as they were walking into the country. And they went back and told the rest, but they did not believe them.

Afterward he appeared to the eleven themselves as they sat at table; and he upbraided them for their unbelief and hardness of heart, because they had not believed those who saw him after he had risen. And he said to them, "Go into all the world and preach the gospel to the whole creation."

This text reminds me of a century ago, when the missionary movement was strong on campuses around the nation. Students were expected literally to "preach the gospel to the whole creation."

He who believes and is baptized will be saved; but he who does not believe will be condemned.

> And these signs will accompany those who believe:
> in my name they will cast out demons; they will
> speak in new tongues; they will pick up serpents,
> and if they drink any deadly thing, it will not hurt
> them; they will lay their hands on the sick, and they
> will recover.
> So then the Lord Jesus, after he had spoken to
> them, was taken up into heaven, and sat down at
> the right hand of God. (Mark 16: 16-19)

And the twentieth verse gets back to the same point. It notes that as Jesus apparently is seated at the right hand of God, the disciples "went forth and preached everywhere, while the Lord worked with them and confirmed the message by the signs that attended it." And then the author adds "Amen."

The Gospel story could have ended at verse eight: "And they went out and fled from the tomb; for trembling and astonishment had come upon them; and they said nothing to anyone, for they were afraid." But thanks be to God, there had already been indications, even in the first verses, that something else was likely to follow. I do not know what happened to Mark during this writing. Perhaps the Spirit brought a fresh anointing on the writer, saying, "There is more, but stop here, so that a little space will be left," leaving people to wonder what happened in that little space.

A promise had been made to the disciples. "Go, tell his disciples and Peter that he is going before you to Galilee; there you will see him, as he told you" (Mark 16:7). And earlier, in the fourteenth verse, there is an indication that afterwards, in Galilee, more things would happen.

Years ago, I would have said that in the little space between verse eight and verse nine, the Lord had anointed the disciples. But because we have said the anointing of the Holy Spirit is that process by which we come to a fundamental awareness of God's appointment, empowerment, and guidance in our calling to the work of the kingdom, it becomes inappropriate to assume what happened in this brief space was the "complete" anointing of the disciples for the work of ministry. It is more appropriate and more consistent with our definition of anointing to say that in that little space, there likely was a continuation of the process of anointing, or additional dimensions of the anointing occurred so that the disciples were then made ready to go forth in the power of the Spirit, as their Lord had done. Who would discount all that went on before that little space in the Gospel and what was to occur later? The anointing already was at work in the disciples as they believed Jesus when he said they were special and every hair on their heads was numbered.

Jesus told the disciples, "You are the salt of the earth. ...You are the light of the world" (Matthew 5: 13-14). He assured them that they were more important than the grass of the field, which is alive today, but tomorrow is thrown into the oven.

Therefore, we should avoid understandings of the anointing that begin with discounting the significance and affirmation of the individual. No, Jesus wasn't about that. Jesus nurtured his disciples. He taught them theory with an added practicum. Again, nurture was a central aspect of Jesus' ministry with the disciples.

Jesus called the disciples to readiness! This was a continual call from the beginning of the disciples' ministry to the event at Calvary. Jesus would say, "Come, let us go over to the other side." He became disappointed at times at how little they seemed to master and comprehend - at how inadequate their preparation seemed to be for the test that life would be sure to issue. They kept flunking out, even in the most elementary aspects of their responsibilities.

Jesus worked with them. He helped them to experience divine approval and gave them signs. God is with you, he would say. He wanted them to know when walking on the water, in the middle of the night - even when they thought they were alone - God was with them. So he encouraged them to believe.

I understand how difficult it must have been for the Gospel writers to record their stories. They wrote to tell us of miracles of how Peter walked on the water, how the dead were resurrected, accounts of how fish were multiplied, and how the sick received their healing. I understand how they must have been baffled by these facts. It may not have been difficult for them to include these incidents in their world view, but it must have been problematic for them to understand how these miracles were performed. It seemed Jesus was constantly showing the disciples there was more power available to them than they realized.

Consider Jesus and the disciples experiencing wilderness periods when they are left alone. Enemies attacked them and challenged them because of their rebellious proclivities. Still, Jesus urged them to bear witness to the truth, even when the threats of others tended to intimidate the disciples into silence. Peter, usually ready to speak out, denied the Lord when his loyalty would have seemed most important.

I understand we cannot discount all of those experiences that the disciples shared with Jesus when we talk about the anointing of the Spirit. So between verses eight and nine and those that follow, it is all right to identify things that happened that "rounded out" the anointing - that added dimensions to it. It seems sometimes we need a booster shot to retain what already has begun to take form

Picture the disciples "at table." When this expression is used, some people may visualize the communion table without realizing the element of the anointing that is taking place in connection with the communion. When we pray, "Lord, bless these elements: this bread, this wine, this cup," do you think the Spirit comes like the four winds and bypasses the broken pieces of humanity to bless and touch the bread and cup and then leave? Oh no!

We remember that Jesus often stopped en route to his destination because what he encountered on the way also needed his touch. So it is at the table, when we pray for the blessing of the elements, the Spirit doesn't ignore the pains deep in the human heart. The Spirit comes prepared to bless everything that is broken. Our acceptance of the invitation to the table is a call to blessing. Our openness should result in the application of a healing balm for our many afflictions. Just as Jesus met them, he also meets us at table.

It should be easy for us to experience the Spirit, to say "yes" and receive. But what if we do not sense such a divine visitation? Does that mean the Spirit is not present? No, this is not something based on our feelings. It is at times when we aren't sure of the Spirit's presence that we should remind ourselves of the faithfulness of God and even if we don't feel anything, we understand the power that enlivens us at table when we say the words of Jesus, "This is my body, broken for you. This is my blood, poured out." And while we may wish we could feel it then, until we do sense the undergirding, we can still live in the truth that our brokenness is healed. And so, in my tradition, although transubstantiation has not been our focus at table, we do claim an experience of the living Christ.

So we can say that in that period between the verses, something happened. Additional dimensions of the anointing were given to the disciples and if we look at the Johannine concept from John's Gospel account we find there was also a kind of empowerment from beyond. This empowerment from beyond involves the capacity of Jesus to stand in their midst in that room and breathe upon them. Ruah, the holy wind, gets around in so many different forms. And Jesus told them to receive the Holy Spirit and the authority that went with it.

I consider it a joy that every tradition need not be measured by the modality of emotional expression of another. I am so happy that God respects our various temperaments. For those of us who can better receive the breathing of the Holy Spirit, a more vigorous form of visitation may not be appropriate. At any rate, God meets us where we are. Thank God we have overcome in our ecumenical conversations our former preoccupations with modes. We now are able to give room to the many different ways by which the Spirit comes to us.

In my tradition and experience, the breathing of the Spirit is more personal. Yet for some it may be difficult to think of anything breathing upon us. Rather than getting bogged down over specific manifestations, we should focus on how we can be empowered as a result of receiving the Spirit.

The anointing is that dimension which continuously provides the oxygen by which all the works of the Spirit are ignited - set on fire to provide energy for activity. So, breathing begins and there's a little flame in the heart. The Spirit fans it, not much, but some. So a little flame begins through the breathing of the Spirit where perhaps too vigorous a visitation could cause it to be extinguished. We preach and lecture and trust that the word of God will fan the flame.

Jesus disclosed to the disciples all of the things he had been trying to share in a summarization at the end of a three-year training course.

Did we hear him say, "Go into all the world and preach the gospel?" "That's what I want you to do." And this day Jesus says to us, "this moment is a time for my resurrection story to become real for you." That I, Jim Forbes, speak the words, knowing precisely where to direct them isn't important. I do not know whether you have been called to this responsibility. But may this be the time when if I say, "Go into all the world and preach the gospel," those to whom God is speaking will hear a direct message. It may be that the Spirit will ring in hearts and minds this day and we will never again doubt it is the word which has come to us. So it can be for us as it was for the disciples when Jesus sat down. They who had been breathed upon went forth and preached everywhere.

Still, there are other dimensions of the anointing for those who can stand the vigor of wind and fire. In Acts, we learn there are additional dimensions to the Spirit's anointing. For some who do not know how to yield to more vigorous expressions, the still, small voice comes. Understanding the various ways the Spirit comes helps us to appreciate how the various traditions, ecumenically speaking, begin to understand that on a particular day, God may come to us in a totally new and different way. We may be reinvigorated and reinspired by expressions of another tradition.

Why must we limit ourselves to a particular pattern of expectation? It is possible to get sick and tired of all fuss and no quiet, or all quiet and no fuss. Why do we lock ourselves into one mode of expression, insisting God must be revealed in a particular form or time? Instead, we should show more concern over whether the signs follow us as believers . . . are we casting out demons, etc.?

I am grateful for Walter Wink's work, *Naming the Powers*, so that moderns, who are always a little afraid of demons, will understand that demons may represent an alien spirit in institutional arrangements that war against the message of God to the church. Demons can rage in nations not with tails and pitchforks, but in manifestations that oppose the kingdom. We who are called upon to be preachers would like to be used by God. One way to do that is to identify the demons that are prowling the streets of our city. In institutions - ecclesiastical, political, and social - the demons play havoc with the peace that has been promised to the people of God. This makes it urgent for us to preach under the anointing so that we can point to and be the signs that do follow. We are to cast out demons. We who live in institutional arrangements where demonic activity is the order of the day can, through the preaching of the word, observe the moaning and groaning of demons as they depart, because that which is greater than the demonic is present in us. Our preaching can evoke that power and be a catalyst for the Spirit to burst in and cast out demons.

Our ecumenical discussion of the anointing can have us speak in new tongues. Now the mention of this gift could cause some to feel uneasy. I myself had trouble receiving the gift of speaking in tongues. But I recall what Carlyle Marney used to say to me, "Jim, no man amounts to much until he learns to bless his own origins." So, thank God, since then, I have experienced this gift. Indeed, many outside of the Pentecostal denomination have come to appreciate this expression as one of the most significant insights of the Pentecostal tradition. However, I am not prepared to say that speaking in tongues is to be totally contained within a particular doctrinal framework.

Indeed, I think that using this experience as the only way of distinguishing those who have been anointed or baptized in the Spirit from those who have not goes beyond the biblical claim. We must respect the freedom and sovereignty of the Spirit and not bind the Spirit to our traditional understandings. I do not stand with those who say, "You didn't speak in tongues; therefore, you don't know anything about the Spirit. You haven't been anointed, or you haven't been baptized." I cannot join in that argument.

I do know that speaking in tongues gets us on our knees to acknowledge things that often need to be said. "I may have no rational capacity to understand all that ought to be said as my expression to God, or to understand all that God is trying to say to me. Speaking in tongues is a way to communicate through the mouth what is in our spirit when we may not have the cognitive resources to do it. It may be that those of you who are sophisticated enough can do it in Latin...but that might leave some of us out. So, speaking in tongues becomes a way of acknowledging there may be something on our hearts, though we don't know how to articulate it."

The issue is broader than linguistics though. It is being able to communicate without pretension of adequate understanding. This is a significant breakthrough for many because if we had to completely understand the matters of the Spirit before we could pray, many of us would be cut off from communicating with the Lord. My message is not to insist that everyone must speak in tongues; however, I will say this: ecumenically the church will lose an opportunity for growth toward the broader frontiers of faith if we forbid the use of this gift. Therefore, as far as I am concerned, if the Spirit gives me the opportunity to speak in tongues, I am glad to affirm it without insisting that everybody else wear it as a badge to be included in the body of Christ.

This gift of tongues is one of the ways we maintain spiritual vitality since the inspired utterance may be more important than that which I am able to articulate out of my own understanding. Furthermore, in terms of communities of faith where the experience of tongues takes place, it is necessary also to have the ability to discern and to have the interpretation of tongues.

Speaking in tongues is only one manifestation of the Spirit's presence, albeit an edifying one. But there are other important dimensions. In this battle, we will have to be able to pick up serpents - not like snake handlers in Appalachia. Our serpents are in the institutions in which we live, work, and serve. Whether the institutions are academic or ecclesiastical, there are serpents there. There is poison there. There is no way to live in our communities without experiencing the bite of the serpent. Let no one fool you. All of the scholars are not saints. All of the bishops are not saints, and all of the ecclesiastical leaders are not necessarily saints. No, there are sinners, serpents, and poison in all of these institutions.

If we seek a situation where there is no poison, where there are no snakes, we have a long journey before us. We require the ability to stand and serve in situations where values are compromised. We need to be able to stand the poison, not taken intentionally, but absorbed just by living in the community, and still not be hurt morally or spiritually.

With the Spirit in our ministry, there will be a laying on of hands so that the sick will recover. When preaching is anointed, people will be healed in the process. This doesn't require a special prayer line. The preached word is sufficient. I am grateful I have had at least one experience in which healing took place during the preaching process.

At the 1974 World Conference on the Holy Spirit in Jerusalem, Kathryn Kuhlman ministered healing. Almost two hundred people claimed their healing in one night. Before the healing service, I had preached the sermon of the evening. Since time was limited, I had to preach quickly. After I finished, Kuhlman ministered healing to others. She told us, "I'm not the healer. It is God who is doing the healing." I was deeply moved by the power of her ministry.

Actually, I was a bit jealous. I felt that being a professor and a preacher was insignificant compared with her extraordinary gifts. Then Kathryn Kuhlman turned around and said to us pastors, "Pastors, you can be healers too if you let the power of God work through you."

I heard her, but to myself I said, "Um hum, sure."

As the benediction was given, a woman and her husband came to the stage. Before I could leave, she said to me, "The Lord led us to come and say something to you. My husband was here, hoping to be touched by Kathryn Kuhlman because he had a hearing problem. He was completely deaf in one ear. You preached," she said, "from the Gospel according to Mark where it says, 'Jesus said, to the man whose ears were closed, "Ephphatha".'

"When you preached and said that word, my husband was waiting for Kathryn so he could be healed. He wanted you to hurry and get out of the way, so he could receive his healing. Then when you said that word, 'Ephphatha,' his ear was opened! The Lord wanted us to come and let you know that even through the preaching of the word, healing can take place."

That was an extraordinary lesson for me. While we may not always have such dramatic experiences, we may find we can be instruments of healing for someone with broken relationships. Perhaps the healing will come to our own hearts when the bitterness that has built up in our lives is cast out. It is my faith that whenever the anointed preaching of the gospel occurs, healing takes place.

Edwin Dargan, in *History of Preaching*, emphasizes that while almost every age had special preachers, the general quality of preaching rarely rose above the spiritual state of the culture at the time. What a keen insight!

There are times when the power of a culture sets limits on what can be imagined and even appropriated. So if we live in a time of death, it is natural to expect death to be present in the preaching. Therefore, in this time and culture so infused with death, how much death there is in preaching. The culture is working to set limits on the possibilities of spiritual transformation.

I am concerned that we who talk about spiritual development often are oblivious to what's going on in our culture.

There is death in the culture that will not help us. But there is also life and signs of life. There are persons in our culture, often unheeded, unheard, and unsung, who provide remnants of life in the midst of an otherwise dead reality. There are writers, painters, musicians, prophets, and poets who may not be members of a church. These holders of the remnants are given eyes to see and skills to speak in words filled with life. They may seem to be speaking in tongues, but something in our hearts responds and says, "Yes, that's it." Musicians can be found who discern what is in the hearts and minds of those who are dead in the valley of dry bones. Writers, painters, and humble workers who have no claim to fame are able to speak words of life.

The angels hear and ask, "May we not use these secular voices and thereby lift them to the sacred as Dante tried to do?" In this way, those who unknowingly are used by God may be given a place, if not in the church, at least in the vestibule, where we entering must pass them. There is a sense in which even a dead culture has voices that may speak truth and stir new life.

An important element in our search for anointed preaching is the church. The seminaries who train the preachers and congregations who spawn them are equally responsible for nurturing the called to a level of grace where others recognize they are anointed. The anointing of prophets and preachers for this age requires seminaries and congregations to work together. Both seminaries and congregations must say, "What we want is anointed preachers, so whatever we can do to be a part of the process, we'll do it. When our energy fails, we will encourage and support those who are able to carry on the work."

When I first started to talk about the work of the

preacher in the congregation I referred to it as the ministry of raising the dead. In that sense, seminary is the place where we prepare people to raise the dead. However, much of the groundwork preparation for this should take place in the students' congregations before they get to these seminaries. Therefore, the preparation is a joint effort of congregation and seminary. If we are going to be a part of the formation of anointed ministers of the word, we must stop quenching the Spirit. We must not stop the Spirit's work just because it challenges our current understanding of ourselves. We encumber the Spirit when we who are supposed to be partners in the business of kingdom, steadily fight what the Spirit tries to move us to do.

If we are going to have anointed ministers of the word, congregations and seminaries will have to commit themselves to the legitimization of the spiritual quest. This may sound obvious to you, but religious institutions are sometimes better at putting on the brakes than accelerating towards the quest for religious depth. If we move too far, we are considered outside of the parameters of the institution's control. When this happens, the institutions will say, "far enough."

Our goal is that institutions and students of ministry will gather these insights that will enable them to discern between what is of the Spirit and what is not of the Spirit. Once the signs of the Spirit are understood, the institution can legitimize the growth of its people. Let it be a cardinal sin worthy of condemnation for preachers, professors, or religious leaders to stop folks from growing spiritually simply because their growth pattern is beyond their limits of control. A good example of what a congregation should be like is Antioch. I love that church at Antioch. If I ever have the privilege of naming a church, I will name it Antioch, even Antioch Episcopal Church. And if the church lived up to its name, it would be a church that believed in the Spirit. That congregation had a Christ-oriented Spirit. The style of their living and worship demonstrated that the Spirit was real in their church. They recognized the gifts the Spirit gave the people. They encouraged one another. They laid hands on all who needed healing. They had a teaching ministry. Love and generosity flourished in that community. They were open to the voice of God as it came through clergy, or the equivalent of clergy in that time, and laity alike. Prophecy was accepted there. They were mature enough to let people speak freely since in the mouth of two or three witnesses will every word be established. Yes, Antioch represents the kind of congregation we need. Even seminaries should be like Antioch in their acknowledgment of the Spirit as present and active.

Both seminaries and congregations must deliberately seek liberation from servitude to the culture and life that is not governed by the Spirit. For our culture is skillful at co-opting all who would be beguiled into serving the world system in the name of the Lord. We must not provide a dwelling place for them. Without caution, churches and seminaries become only the safety valves for the culture. That's why some people whose allegiances are to earthly kingdoms sometimes fund us. They fund churches and seminaries because "y'all keep the natives happy and siphon off creative discontent."

Seminaries and churches are viewed by certain elements of the culture as essential in helping keep obscure and removed to a plane of mysticism the differences in values, power, and resources that exist between groups in the culture. Seminaries and churches that are weak in the Spirit do that. Developing anointed preachers and being the safety valve for society cannot be done at the same time by a congregation or seminary. Therefore, churches *and* seminaries must pray for liberation from being co-opted into servitude. They must prevent the stifling of prophetic imagination in preachers whom God has called to be in ministry, called to raise the dead.

We must offer ourselves as agents for the cultivation of a renewed spirit in our sacred vocations as pastors. How sinful it would be for a church or seminary to tamper with the Holy Spirit's effort to bring forth a new person for a vocation of ministry. This would be true even if the shape of the person's vocation is different from the one we imagine for ourselves.

If I were to tamper with the Spirit's desire, and try to bend a Christian education teacher into a professional preacher, I would be in error. If a student is called to a ministry of social work and I try to remold the student into my ecclesiastical scheme, I am wrong. I may want all of the bright students to pursue my field, but if I lure them to it solely to get credit for producing great students, I may be interfering with the Spirit who is trying to develop this person for the vocation that God intends.

To be a catalyst in the development of anointed ministers, we must have deep respect for the many expressions of the Spirit's work. Sometimes through a kind of eschatological epistemology, a kind of knowing that is not produced by our rational faculties, we must dare to tilt toward the kingdom, even at risk of institutional inconvenience.

We need, in churches and seminaries, to recover the tension between institutional necessity and the demands of the kingdom. If we break the tension, we shirk our responsibility and deny our sacred trust. We must live and move within the tension.

We may even have to consent to a worldwide clergy factory recall. All Christian clergy: Pentecostals, Baptists, Presbyterians, Methodists, Congregationalists, Roman Catholics, Orthodox, and all the rest may need to be recalled. Something has fallen into disrepair in too many of us, which we will not recover until we go back to the factory, back to the altar of grace. We need not ask, "What's wrong with me?" My carburetor may be clogged and my brakes may be defective. But whatever is needed to pull the church together, to empower our clergy, and address the needs of our time, must be done. We must move with the Spirit's effort to anoint us, and call us again and again to reaffirmation.

We need to pray, "Lord, you anointed me, and I want reinvestitures." As we discover where our weaknesses lie, let us come before the Lord and say, "Lord, you did something for me years ago that helped me to rise above my preoccupation with my own interests. Do that again."

For all of us to be revitalized in our time, we are going

to have to find a way to get light from dark corners. We must point to the light others carry and say, "There! That's what I'm talking about! Look over there, too. There is light!" We must cultivate an appreciation for more than our own way. The Lord hears the prayers that have been prayed for unity. Jesus said, "Lord, make them one."

I can imagine a conversation between an angel and the Lord.

"I have a suggestion for how your churches might be one," says the angel.

"What is your suggestion, angel?"

The angel replies, "If we can determine which spiritual aspect is lacking in a particular tradition, and plant that element in an opposite tradition, even if it is a tradition the other tradition disagrees with, the one lacking will develop a hunger for the additional dimension and cry out, 'Oh God, give me that additional dimension.'"

"Then we will be able to take the message to the first tradition, and say, 'The Lord hath heard your prayer and says what you have requested has been granted. When they ask where the blessing is to be found, we can say, 'In that group you detest the most. To that crowd you so often believe holds no truth at all.'"

Such a conversation would point to the irony and beauty of a pluralistic society. All of us need to understand there are some things God is not going to give directly to white people. There are some things black folk have that white folk desperately need. There are some things that white folk have that black folk need to pursue their fulfillment. Men and women of whatever color need the gifts and perspectives of each other. So it is that you cannot be fulfilled without me and I cannot be fulfilled without you.

We, as committed members of the clergy and laity, must therefore find a way to confess our debt. We must cry out to God for light. We must get on the path of obedience, regardless of whether we feel that any strange palpitations of heart have taken place. We must seek confirmation and encouragement - pray without ceasing

103

and serve without fainting, even in hard times. And if anybody wants the blessing of additional dimensions of growth, it can be found in the experience of Holy Spirit anointing.

When I talk about the anointing, I am talking about appropriating what is offered to us. I am calling us to claim it, live by it, and dare to express to God, "It's a part of my heritage as a member of Christ's body. Please don't deny me, Lord. I want all of those things that are necessary for me to be faithful."

I see signs that the Holy Spirit is now at work. The churches and institutions where we serve have the opportunity to serve at a deeper level. Are we ready to be used by the Spirit to revitalize the body? Will we assist in promoting the anointing, through God's Spirit, of the world, so that the society can overcome death and come to life again? Each seminary and each congregation has to answer for itself.

When we finally say "no" to the death within us and around us and cry out to God, "Lord, we cannot be content until revitalization, a Jubilee, comes to us," I believe it will happen.

Let me share this true story about when I was trying to decide what I should do vocationally. I had a dream where I went to a church meeting and met my friends. As they were going out of the church, my friends passed me, not recognizing who I was.

I said, "Where are you guys going?"

They answered, "We are going to Jim Forbe's funeral."

"He has died?" I asked in disbelief. Then I said, "Let me go with you."

I traveled with them and saw the church with all the people gathered for my funeral. As they were filing by, looking at Jim Forbes, some would say, "He doesn't look too bad for his age. Look at him lying there in the coffin." And I too went toward the coffin and sadly looked at him. With a strange distant feeling, I returned to my seat.

Then the minister said rather abruptly, "These services are over. The interment will be right here." The mortician then came forward and started to lower the lid of the coffin, which began to turn into my bed. I shouted at the top of my voice, "I object! I object! I object!"

Brothers and sisters, there's death in the land. There's death in ourselves, in our preaching, and in our institutions. But through the anointing power of the Holy Spirit, we must object and cry out to God, "Renew your people now!"

BIBLIOGRAPHY

Brilioth, Yngve T. *A Brief History of Preaching*. Translated by Karl E. Mattson. Philadelphia: Fortress Press, 1965.

Burge, Gary M. *The Anointed Community: The Holy Spirit in the Johannine Tradition*. Grand Rapids, Mich.: William B. Eerdmans Pub. Co., 1987.

Bushnell, Horace. *Christian Nurture*. New York: Charles Scribner, 1861.

Buttrick, George A. *Jesus Came Preaching: Christian Preaching in the New Age*. New York: Charles Scribner's Sons, 1932.

Chappell, Clovis Gillham. *Anointed to Preach*. Nashville, Tenn.: Abingdon-Cokesbury Press, 1951.

Dargan, Edwin. *A History of Preaching*. Grand Rapids, Mich.: Baker Book House, 1954.

Dupre, Louis. "Spiritual Life in a Secular Age." *Religion and America: Spiritual Life in a Secular Age*. Edited by Mary Douglas and Steven M. Tipton. Boston: Beacon Press, 1983.

Eichrodt, Walter. *Ezekiel: A Commentary*. Translated by Cosslett Quin. Philadelphia: Westminster Press, 1970.

Forbes, James A., Jr. "Pentecostalism and the Renewal of the Church." B. Div. thesis, Union Theological Seminary, 1962.

Fosdick, Henry. "God of Grace and God of Glory." *Pilgrim Hymnal*. Boston: Pilgrim Press, 1960.

The Holy Bible, Thompson Chain-Reference Bible (KJV). Fourth Improved Edition. Compiled and edited by

Frank Charles Thompson. Indianapolis, Ind.: B. B. Kirkbride Bible Co., 1964.

The Interpreter's Bible. Volume 7: General Articles on the New Testament; The Gospel According to St. Matthew; The Gospel According to St. Mark. Nashville, Tenn.: Abingdon-Cokesbury, 1951.

Massey, James Earl. *The Sermon in Perspective: The Sermon in Perspective: A Study of Communication and Charisma*. Grand Rapids, Mich.: Baker Book House, 1976.

Moltmann, Jurgen. *Theology of Hope: On the Ground and the Implications of a Christian Eschatology*. Translated by James W. Leitch. New York: Harper & Row, 1967.

Moltmann, Jurgen. *The Crucified God: The Cross of Christ as the Foundation and Criticism of Christian Theology*. Translated by R. A. Wilson and John Bowden. New York: Harper & Row, 1974.

Moltmann, Jurgen. *The Church in the Power of the Spirit: A Contribution to Messianic Ecclesiology*. Translated by Margaret Kohl. New York: Harper & Row, 1977.

Moon, Jesse K. "The Holy Spirit in Preaching." *Paraclete* 2 (Fall 1977): 27.

The New Oxford Annotated Bible, Revised Standard Version. New York: Oxford University Press, 1977.

Newbigin, Lesslie. *The Household of God: Lectures on the Nature of the Church*. New York: Friendship Press, 1954.

Otto, Rudolf. *The Idea of the Holy: An Inquiry into the Non-rational Factor in the Idea of the Divine and Its Relation to the Rational*. Translated by John W. Harvey. New York: Oxford University Press, 1958.

Pannenberg, Wolfhart. *Christian Spirituality*. Philadelphia: Westminster Press, 1983.

Tillich, Paul. "Spiritual Presence." *The Eternal Now*. New York: Scribner, 1963.

Tillich, Paul. *Systematic Theology*. Vol. 3: Life and the Spirit; History and the Kingdom of God. Chicago: University of Chicago Press, 1963.

Van Dusen, H. Pitney. "Pentecostalism: The Third Force in Christendom." *Life*, June 1958.

Van Dusen, H. Pitney. *Spirit, Son, and Father: Christian*

Faith in the Light of the Holy Spirit. New York: Scribner, 1958.

Wink, Walter. *Naming the Powers: The Language of Power in the New Testament.* Philadelphia: Fortress Press, 1984.

The Holy Spirit and Preaching

Audiocassettes

Now, you can hear, share, and enjoy the powerful sermons exactly as they were delivered by Dr. James Forbes at the prestigious Lyman Beecher Lectures, Yale University.

As the preacher at one of America's most well-known pulpits, Riverside Church, New York City, Dr. Forbes has a strong sense of the need to be "anointed by the Holy Spirit" when he preaches. In four sixty-minute audiocassettes Dr. Forbes inspires and informs clergy and laity about the centrality of the Holy Spirit in preaching.

These tapes can be used at home, at work, in your car, or while you jog!